Revelation Revealed

Volume One

Dr. David Del Vecchio
With Diane Briley

DR. DAVID DEL VECCHIO with DIANE BRILEY

Revelation Revealed: Volume One

© 2022 by Dr. David Del Vecchio with Diane Briley

All rights reserved.

This book is protected under the copyright laws of the United States of America. This book may not be copied or reprinted for commercial gain or profit. The use of short quotations or occasional page copying for personal, or group study is permitted and encouraged. Permission will be granted upon request. Unless otherwise indicated, Scripture quotations are from the King James Version of the Bible.

Dr. David Del Vecchio
Christ Church International
P.O. 5987
Dothan, Al 36302

Translations Quoted:

NIV — New International Version, Copyright © 1973, 1978, 1984 by International Bible Society, Zondervan Publishing House. Used by Permission

NKJV — New King James Version, Copyright © 1982, Thomas Nelson, Inc. Used by Permission

AMP — Scripture quotations taken from the AMPLIFIED BIBLE, Copyright © 1954, 1958, 1962, 1964, 1965, 1987 by The Lockman Foundation. Used by permission. (www.Lockman.org)

HCSB- Scripture quotations marked HCSB are taken from the Holman Christian Standard Bible®, Copyright © 1999, 2000, 2002, 2003, 2009 by Holman Bible Publishers. Used by permission. Holman Christian Standard Bible®, Holman CSB®, and HCSB® are federally registered trademarks of Holman Bible Publishers.

TABLE OF CONTENTS

FORWARD 4

AUTHOR'S NOTE 6

PREFACE 7

INTRODUCTION... 10

A VISION OF SUPERNATURAL PROPORTIONS 24

JESUS IN THE MIDST OF THE EPHESUS CHURCH 53

THE AMERICAN CHURCH 72

SMYRNA: A CHURCH OF SPIRITUAL RICHES 80

PERGAMUM: FAITHFUL YET WORLDLY 91

THYATIRA: THE LOST CHURCH... 108

SARDIS: ALIVE, YET DEAD... 118

PHILADELPHIA: AN OPEN DOOR 131

LAODICEA: A LUKEWARM PEOPLE...138

THE THRONE IN HEAVEN..155

THE SCROLL AND THE LAMB..175

THE SEALS 187

THE 144,000 SEALED.. 210

THE SEVENTH SEAL AND THE GOLDEN CENSER 235

THE TRUMPETS CONTINUE...263

DR. DAVID DEL VECCHIO with DIANE BRILEY

FORWARD

David Del Vecchio has been my friend and student for many years. I have regularly been a guest in the pulpit of Christ Church International where he serves as Senior Minister. David is a serious student of the Word and an accomplished expositor.

In *Revelation Revealed* he has shown some of the exegetical and hermeneutical skills he has developed over the years. This is not a book for scholars only; it is also a book for every man. Its design is to make the most difficult book of the New Testament understandable for the man or woman in the pew. David writes much as he teaches, directly and clearly, warmly, and compassionately. If you will read *Revelation Revealed* with an open Bible and an open heart, you will hear its ever-contemporary message of God's faithfulness in every situation of life.

This is a chapter-by-chapter exposition of the Bible's last book, its grand finale. But it is also the passionate heart message of this servant of God. Will you agree with all this writer's interpretations and conclusions in this book? It is not likely. However, *Revelation Revealed* will open your eyes and quicken your spirit to the greatness of God and His loving-kindness to all His creation.

I recommend *Revelation Revealed* to every thinking Christian.

Ronald E. Cottle, *Ph.D., Ed.D., D.D.*
Founder: Christian Life School of Theology Global
Founder and President Emeritus, Embassy College

DR. DAVID DEL VECCHIO with DIANE BRILEY

AUTHOR'S NOTE

To say I am the author of this book is to deny all the scholars I have heard, and whose works I have read over the period from 1981 until the present, including Dr. Ron Cottle, Dr. Hilton Sutton, Charles Barclay, Kittle, Frederich, R.C. Sproul, Lenski, Kenneth Wuest, and the list goes on. This is a compilation of what I have learned over this period as I sought answers to all the questions I have had about Revelation. I never had any intention of writing a book until I realized the church needed to understand these truths. And for that reason, I write this book.

PREFACE

Do you have questions about the end times and what it will look like? Have you ever had questions about the millennial reign or the rapture? Do you believe in the pre-trib, post-trib, or the rapture? Are you unsure what you believe? This book will help you understand where we are in our world today in reference to the end times.

In an effort to help you understand the various positions people take regarding the Millennial Reign, here are some questions that we should be asking. What is the millennium? When does it take place? What happens during this time? Who does it affect? Is it supported by Scripture?

Throughout this Book, many questions will be answered regarding the Millennium and the great tribulation, such as, why would the number 1000 suddenly need to be literal, especially when it appears 19 times as symbolic, not actual? The term 1000 is used 19 times in Revelation as a symbolic number. How did just 144,000 make it? What if one or two had a change of heart? Is there no room for them? How did the exact number of 144,000 get reached? We read they never lied; did they ever cheat, steal, murmur, slander, behave with pride, arrogance, or even kill? Did they ever give or take offense, and if not, how were they so perfect, since Christ is the only one who was ever perfect? Why just 144,000 men? Why exclude women? Why would God allow the devil to have another 1000 years? Why would someone think that God is going to give Satan another shot at the apple for another 1000 years? What would be the purpose? Do we need a redo? Does all this mean that no one will be left on the earth? If that's the case, where does Satan get the people he will tempt and try for 1000 years? Is God supposed to create some more folks on the earth or send some back? Does that mean we have to rewrite the Bible so that a millennium can fit in it? The resurrection of Jesus defeated Satan so why start all over again? Who will die for this second group? Who do we judge when we are in the new heaven and new earth? To believe in two separate second comings creates a conundrum. How and when do we go, and in which second coming do we go? How can those who die in the so-called millennium be saved?

Answers to these questions, and many more, are found within these pages. As you investigate, study, and read through the content, may Holy Spirit speak to your heart and bring revelation to your life.

DR. DAVID DEL VECCHIO with DIANE BRILEY

INTRODUCTION

Have you ever had questions about the Book of Revelation? Have you tried to read it, study it, and just get confused as you attempt to understand the content and vision that John portrays? Have you had a desire to explore and gain insight as to what John actually saw, or to learn the spiritual concepts within his vision?

If you answered yes to any of these questions, then this Book is for you. I know there are many views and many interpretations of the Book of Revelation, and I for one do not have all the answers. But my prayer for you, the reader, is that you will gain a better understanding as you embark along this journey of studying verse by verse the concepts, experiences, and revelations that John scribes for Jesus as he experienced in his vision.

The book of Revelation has been a topic of much controversy, and because of our finite thinking, it is hard to wrap the concepts, thoughts, and purposes around what God is revealing in this book. Over the course of time, many scholars have devised four different viewpoints of the book: the Preterist View, the Historical View, the Allegorical View, and the Futuristic View. Each view has its own concepts, interpretations, and approach it takes of Revelation.

The **Preterist view** sees events and visions of John as belonging to the past. This view is not corroborated by what John saw or said; Revelation is based upon the prophetic view that John writes about. John even says so in Revelation 1:3 when he says *"prophecy"*. Prophecy is future.

The **Historical view** is a panoramic view of history from the first century to the second coming of Christ. However, history does not substantiate this view, because many of the events John writes about have not yet occurred.

The **Allegorical view** is seen as allegorical, symbolic. It portrays the continuing saga between good and evil throughout history.

And the final view, the **Futuristic view** sees Revelation as it deals with end time events; that is the view many of us have. This view says the events are not as much in John's day, or as historical events, as much as things connected to the second coming of Christ. The correct view of Revelation is past, present, and future. This book is alive and for today.

The origin of the word *revelation* comes from the Greek Word, *apokalupsis*, meaning *to take the cover off*. It is an uncovering or an unveiling of the glory of Christ, and the events of the future.

As we approach the concepts and designs within this book, my prayer is that Holy Spirit will reveal Himself to you in a fresh new way, and the revelation of John's vision will come alive within you like never before.

Revelation 1:1 (NIV) reveals, *"The revelation from Jesus Christ, which God gave him to show his servants what must soon take place. He made it known by sending his angel to his servant John."* This says that the book is the revelation, the uncovering or revealing of Jesus.

Some scholars believe the Apostle John did not write the book of Revelation, because the language used is different than John's other writings. I believe the language was given as Jesus gave it and is done purposely. John is simply being used as the PEN OF JESUS, the amanuensis, writing what Jesus says in His words, revealing what He wants the world to see and know. These writings were written exactly as Jesus revealed them to John, they were NOT John's thoughts or machinations.

The book has also been referred to as the revelation of John or John's Apocalypse, but neither is right. This book of God was given to John to write and reveal Jesus the anointed One of God. John is writing what Jesus is revealing to him to write. Simply said, this is the composition of Jesus, His body, His words, His writings, and His facts. None of this is John's idea or scheme or plan, including the language and the words that have been chosen for the Book of Revelation.

Imagine with me John at the last supper, reclining on the chest of Jesus, he was casual, relaxed, and confident in his master and dearest friend. Now, see John with the vision being revealed to him of who this Lord is and how awesome is this spectacular God, who is no longer seen as John once saw Him.

Mysteries and Symbols

Revelation is a book of both promise and judgment. A promise for those who have been sealed through Christ, and a judgment for Satan and all who refuse Christ. It is filled with the mysteries of God that are intertwined throughout the book, though we may not understand them, the mysteries are revealed in His timing. The times and seasons are left up to Him, and He determines what is revealed and what is kept hidden.

Because we are finite creatures with limited understanding, we are always looking for an explanation of who, what, how and why, but here we are not given everything, because we would make it appear in our finite minds as much less than it really is — and we would ruin the realities of Christ and minimalize His awesomeness, and even lose what He intends to bring us, and where He intends to take us.

The Book of Revelation can produce in us an uncertainty, a sense of being overwhelmed, and a fear of the unknown as everything we see, know, and have become is coming to a final end. This book is filled with a final and symbolic language, referencing figures and symbols that are not to be translated in literal equivalents, as if we can explain everything away in accordance to man's very insignificant and incomplete understanding. Then, eternity looms over us, and we have very few definitive answers, so, with our finite thinking, we try to come up with answers, but at best our answers are often petty and trite.

Some symbols are things never seen or made before; accept the fact that God has much more to reveal, and we will know when He chooses to reveal it. An example is the word locusts or grasshoppers in *Revelation 9:7-10*. Many writers try to compare them with what they see today—that is absolutely foolish and irrelevant. Can we just agree that God will produce something we have not yet seen? After all, He is the God of creation. These creatures even have a king from hell that reigns over them. He comes out of the abyss and leads them.

In the end, we have no clue. **They are symbolic of something not seen on the earth before**—period. For us to translate Revelation as something literal with our limited knowledge and understanding serves no purpose. It is left up to us to trust God to reveal when and what He wishes.

Some of the symbolic language is beyond us and some of the symbols are unearthly. That means they are not of this world, and some are even monstrous. To try to conjure what they represent is futile and counterproductive. God's design of this is to make a bold and powerful impression and that is enough for now. Any translation into the literal will make what has been revealed to John seem weaker than its reality. What John has put into human words, is an attempt to put into human words what is not understood by humanity, because it is still ethereal [from the heavens]. What God has veiled is still veiled, and what He intends to unveil is openly revealed, so that the reader is left with its powerful impression.

Revelation is not a series of parables or spooky unknown information; it is a picture full of mystery, much of it is to be known, while much of it still needs to remain hidden as a mystery. Those who are to know are those who remain firm and persevere to the end.

The focus of this book is the end of time and the revelation of eternity. How can a man's words explain eternity to a finite mind—it cannot. God made the revelation known by sending his angel to his servant John.

"The revelation from Jesus Christ, which God gave him to show his servants what must soon take place" Revelation 1:1 (NIV 2011). Some commentators and teachers have said, "*must come shortly or must take place soon*", means that events have already taken place. That view as we have already discussed is the preterist view.

A view that says the events prophesied by John occurred shortly after John wrote about them. They say that John wrote about things that happened in his lifetime or in the lifetime of the people in the churches to which he was writing. There is a problem with that view; Jesus said He was coming quickly. "*Look, I am coming quickly! [SUDDENLY!] The one who keeps the prophetic words of this book is blessed*" (Revelation 22:7 HCSB). The word *quickly* is the same Greek word that is translated 'shortly' or 'soon' in chapter one. If that is true, then all of these things have already taken place; Christ has already come and there is no hope and no future for us, just death. This verse should be understood to mean that these events would occur soon, as God sees soon, in His timetable.

Have you heard the saying that we are not to know the times and seasons?

The Scripture in *Acts 1:7* (KJV) states, *"And he said unto them, it is not for you to know the times or the seasons, which the Father hath put in his own power."* This verse may need some clarity. The King James translates the word "seasons," but other translations, say *periods or dates*. Other translations are better about this than the KJV, such as the NIV which reads, *"Jesus said to them: It is not for you to know the times or dates the Father has set by His own authority"*, and then the HCSB, which refers to *"times or periods that the Father has set by his own authority."*

I believe we are to know the seasons we are in, not the times and dates, that are known only to God, but the seasons, just as we know what season of the year we are in, and what seasons the church has passed through and is now in. The Bible records that we know the seasons by what we see, so that verse must need more understanding.

The word used here for "times" is *chronos*, which is the *passing of moments or events*. The word for "seasons" is *kairos*, referring to *seasons and times of accomplishments*. That can mean seasons, but more often the word *kairos* is translated as *an occasion, a specific time or occasion or event.*

We are told in Matthew 24, throughout the entire chapter to watch the time and the seasons for the end, and that we would know by what we see that the end is near. There is no argument with the word, just a better and more accurate translating of the word *kairos*.

It is important to study the Word, so that we understand the intent and meaning of God's words, especially when there is an issue that seems to create a question.

Super-Natural

When John writes that he was in the Spirit, he was saying that his natural man was not in the way of his visions. On the contrary, his mental faculties were heightened, and he was able to go beyond his normal abilities to see, hear, and write because of it. *Romans 8:26* (HCSB) states, *"In the same way the Spirit also joins to help in our weakness, because we do not know what to pray for as we should, but the Spirit Himself intercedes for us with unspoken groanings."*

The Greek word for "intercedes" is *huperenthugchano*, which means *beyond normal*; when in the Spirit, we are above normal. John is operating way above normal, because his Spirit is joined with Holy Spirit and his natural ability to see, hear, understand, and write are now way above normal. God is not going to entrust this book that records the end to a natural man and expect him to be able to handle the supernatural; it takes a man filled with the Spirit for him to be able to experience what John experienced. There is no way that John could have received these visions unless God's Spirit joined with his to enhance his natural abilities.

History

Prior to Apostle John's exile to the island of Patmos, Emperor Titus ruled. Little is known about Titus, except for the expelling of the Jews from Jerusalem, because of their behavior and rebellion, and his rebuilding of Rome after it burned. Titus ruled for two years as Emperor, and it's believed that his brother Domitian was involved in his death.

Upon the death of Titus, his brother Domitian, ruled. He was one of the most evil, demented persecutors of the church. History records him as being as evil as Nero and Caligula. Domitian ruled from 81 A.D. to 96 A.D. Before Domitian's death, he granted permission to the proconsul of Asia to place the Apostle John in exile on the Island of Patmos. Just how long he was there, no one knows. That is how we know when the revelation of John was written.

On a certain Sunday in the year of 95 A.D., the Apostle John received the Lord's order to write Revelation. I do not think this vision could have taken place in only one day. His visions were occurring all at the same time. John did not write all that he saw and heard as he stated in *Revelation 10:4 (HCSB)*, *"Seal up what the seven thunders have said and do not write it down."*

John was commanded to write much of it as shown in *Revelation 1:19, 14:13, and 19:9*. It would appear that he wrote as he watched and heard what was occurring in his visions. Some of what he saw and heard went with him to his grave.

As you venture into the book of Revelation, may God truly open your eyes to see what John saw, to experience what he experienced, and understand what the Spirit was saying to him. May the revelation become life changing for you in the midst of the mysteries and symbols of the supernatural.

DR. DAVID DEL VECCHIO with DIANE BRILEY

A VISION OF SUPERNATURAL PROPORTIONS

CHAPTER 1

As the revelation began to unfold, surrounded by heavenly aura; John encountered the most significant presence he had ever experienced. His desperation to understand what was taking place was very evident as he revealed the vision. *Revelation 1:1 (NIV 2011)* tells us, *"The revelation was from Jesus, which God gave him to show his servants what must soon take place."* It was important for John to establish from the beginning that this revelation was not from him, it was <u>not</u> just another dream; it was so much more. God revealed what was coming for His servants through John's vision. Jesus' purpose was not to scare the church with the contents of the vision, but to prepare the church. The message of this revelation was so important that Jesus sent an angel to John to testify about everything he saw. So, not only did Jesus establish this vision on earth for the church, but he also established the vision in the heavenly realm through the witness of the angel.

Have you ever told a story that someone else told you, and made sure you explained to those listening that you did not generate the story? You made it clear someone else told it to you. This is the same for John, as he began, he wanted to make it clear that the revelation and visions were not from him. He was merely a conduit, a scribe, being used by the Spirit of God to bring forth a revelation directly from Jesus. Jesus established through John that everything getting ready to take place was a testimony of Jesus. It was the Word of God.

In the history of the church, many have taught the Book of Revelation was a book in the Bible that was to be avoided. Avoidance happens in many cases, because people do not understand the content, context, and meaning of the revelation

John describes, however, those who embrace it are given a promise to be blessed. Jesus explains this in *Revelation 1:3 (NIV 2011)*, *"Blessed is the one who reads aloud the words of this prophecy, and blessed are those who hear it and take to heart what is written in it, because the time is near."* His focus is on blessing and preparing His people.

Validity of Authorship

John's role in the delivery of this revelation is vitally important. Jesus needed a scribe who could articulate exactly what he was seeing and hearing and be able to communicate it to the people. Jesus told John that the revelation was given by the Father to Me, and I am giving it to you, to share with the believers; just as you see it and hear it, you give it to them.

Jesus needed to make sure the person He chose to deliver the revelation for the church was someone who could be trusted. He did not need someone who would boast about being chosen but would simply be a messenger making sure the church knew Jesus was the author. You see, if those reading the book of

Revelation view it as though John was the producer of the visions, then everything written loses its power, because it simply becomes a dream. But, for those who read it as it was intended, the actual Word of God, seeing it as Jesus is revealing it, then it brings forth the power of the anointing that God intended. So, when the reader reads every word, it is as though the words jump off the page and become life.

Jesus established his authorship in *Revelation 1:4-5 (NIV)* where he addresses seven churches and explains that this is from, *"Him who is, and who was, and who is to come, from the seven spirits before His throne, and from Jesus Christ, who is the faithful witness, the firstborn from the dead, and the ruler of the kings of the earth."* He continues down to verse 8, where He says, *"I am the Alpha and the Omega, says the Lord God, who is, and who was, and who is to come, the Almighty."* Jesus designated Himself by sealing the prophecy with the authority of His name. The Alpha and the Omega, the first and the last letters of the Greek alphabet, declare that God is everything from A to Z, thus in control of all history with a power that is absolute.

In viewing the terms *Alpha and Omega* that John uses, we can understand the intention of the vision. These terms help us establish that the vision was given in the Greek language, because if John would have written, "I am the *Alepth* and the *Tau*," we would know it was given in the Hebrew language. During this time, the Greek language was the most commonly used, which meant more people than not, would be able to read it and understand it, and by using the most common language of the day meant that this revelation was for everyone, both the Jews and the Gentiles. John did not even transcribe the vision into his native language, Aramaic, which was the language Jesus spoke when He was here. I believe if Jesus meant for this message to be only for the Jews, He would have had John write it in Aramaic. But Jesus' purpose was far bigger than one group of people; he meant it for the entire world to hear.

As Jesus began to address each of the churches with warnings, encouragement, edification, direction, and correction, He needed to provide a hope to all believers, which

He successfully accomplished when He said in *Revelation 1:8*, *"I am the One who is coming"* (Paraphrased).

He also needed to establish who He was, and His purpose as reflected in *Revelation 19:13 (NIV)*, where Jesus states that *His name is the Word of God, Logos*. By setting this precedence, it gave credence to John's obedience to function as the amanuensis for Jesus and establish with the churches the validity of the prophecy they were about to embark upon.

Some scholars believe a different John wrote Revelation, because the style is not consistent with John's other writings, but this belief is not true. The reason for the difference in style of writing is because John merely penned what Jesus revealed to Him, making Jesus the author of the Book of Revelation, written in Jesus' tone and style.

The Bigger Picture

John reminded the churches that there is a bigger picture. All of the suffering, endurance, and trials they have been experiencing are all for a greater cause and will not last forever. Jesus told John in *Revelation 1:6* to encourage the churches for they were made to be *kings and priests* (some interpretations state *kingdom of priests*) so they could serve Him *(Paraphrased)*.

The precedence Jesus established here was completely different than the culture of the day where kings reigned over kingdoms and priests ministered in the house of God. Jesus' precedence was astronomical, as He revealed that His servants were made to be kings and priests, *not servants*. His use of terminology of kings and priests in this cultural setting revealed that kings and priests were set apart and reserved as very special, important people; the very elite.

We are the literal house of God, the temple of Holy Spirit, and we have been called to minister to Him in this house, but not as servants. Jesus said to John that we are kingly priests, and we have been called by Jesus to be heavenly royalty. When we grasp that concept and actually believe it, we will function from a position of victory and not defeat. We are not at that place yet, but that is God's plan for us.

So many times, we are just like the churches that Jesus is addressing where the circumstances we face are beyond our control, and we give in to the trials, tribulations, and sufferings of life. We lose our focus, especially when we receive a bad report. Have you ever received a phone call with bad news, or got involved in a situation that appeared very bad? What did you do? How did you handle it? Did you believe the bad report, or give in to the situation? We often quote, "Whose report will you believe? We will believe the report of the Lord." Yet in the midst of those bad situations, we do the opposite. At the time of the phone call, or in the midst of a situation is when we win or lose the battle believing what the Word says, and not what the caller has told us. This is very evident, when we receive a bad report by a doctor. Before we know it, we are agreeing with him proclaiming the words as we share with others grasping for help. We reveal our fear to the enemy, and he picks it up and runs with it. This is the time to say out loud, "Devil, I do not accept this evil report, I choose to believe what God said, He is my healer, and my protector. I am not denying the doctor's facts, I simply deny its right to stay on me or on someone I love, so I refuse to receive it." *Ephesians 4:27* tells us to, *"Give no place to the devil" (Paraphrased).* We must stand in faith and accept what God wants while denying the package the enemy sent.

Numbers 13 provides a beautiful example of how it should work. Moses called forth 12 spies to go and spy out the land. When they returned to Moses, ten of them said, *"We are not able to take the land, it looks too big for us" (Numbers 13:27, Paraphrased).* When they said it, the words hit God's ears and He said, *"That is an evil report of unbelief and they have just admitted to me that they have more faith in the devil than they do in Me, now they will remain in this desert."* They believed what they saw *over* what God said. Yet, two of the spies, Caleb and Joshua brought back a different report, they believed and said, *"We are well able to take the land" (Numbers 13:27, Paraphrased).* When God heard this, He said to the world, *"Give them what they want, what they have just said with the words out of their own mouths."* Caleb and Joshua used the currency accepted in heaven, FAITH.

They truly believed that they could conquer the land and stood on it, resulting in a victory for everyone. Just like Joshua and Caleb, you can have what you say just as *Mark 11:22-24* tells us. When we see ourselves as kings and priests in God's kingdom, we have the ability to overcome any situation, because of *Whose* we are. We do not face any situation alone; God is always with us walking us through with Holy Spirit. The choice is ours just as it was for the seven churches. We have to choose to turn our attention on the Kingdom and see ourselves as kings and priests. Our situations will not last forever. There is an end to our circumstances and current situations, an end to all this enduring as Matthew stated, *"but the one who stands firm to the end will be saved" (Matthew 24:13 NIV)*. John encourages us, just as he did those who were part of the seven churches to direct our attention on praise to God always. We are part of the kingdom of God right now, here on planet earth. We are the kingdom that the world opposes, and we are as John said, kings and priests to serve Jesus and His Father, God.

Isle of Patmos

John was an ordinary person, a follower of Jesus, and a disciple. It was important to him to make sure that everyone knew that he was simply a scribe for Jesus. He didn't want anyone to think what he was presenting was coming from him. One of the ways John accomplished this task was to reference himself as a brother and companion as he addressed the seven churches. He took the time to establish where he was, and what day it was, when he began his first vision. He basically told them he was a personal witness of what was taking place as he gave an account of what he heard and saw from Jesus in visions while on the Isle of Patmos.

The Isle of Patmos was used by Rome to exile those who were an upper class of lawbreakers and those who offended the emperor. The island itself was about 10 miles long and 6 miles broad and mostly rocky. This is where Emperor Domitian sent John into exile.

Some scholars believe John was living in exile in a cave on the Isle of Patmos at the time he saw the visions and wrote Revelation, while others thought maybe he went to the island on a missionary journey. However, there were few people on the island, and an entire world of lost people on the mainland.

John, as a follower of Christ, understood what his brothers and sisters in Christ were enduring. He understood the sufferings and the endurance it took to overcome those sufferings as John wrote in Revelation 1:9, *"All of us share with Christ in suffering, in the kingdom, and in patience to continue"* (paraphrased). The word for "patience" is better translated as *patient endurance*. Here he does not mean *quietly waiting*, but more of *endurance*. The Greek word for "endurance" is *Hupomone* from the word *Hupomeno*, meaning *cheerful endurance; waiting under trial while we anticipate coming up out of the trial as victors*. Much like a horse coming out of battle with his front legs pumping the air in excitement. Through the battle he has been standing victorious and now he shows it. He expected to win, but he knew he would have to wait to reveal it until the end.

Notice John writes three words in succession that seem unrelated. The words are suffering, kingdom, and patient endurance, so why did he put kingdom between suffering and patient endurance? Why put kingdom between these two words? Because as saints, we are in the kingdom, and part of being in the kingdom is suffering and endurance.

Throughout history, we can see the lives of many who suffered for the cause of Christ. An example is that of Mother Theresa, who was a living martyr. She was not killed by some lunatic for her faith – but she died daily for the cross of Christ and lived only for His cause.

Each day of her life was the day a martyr lived for the cause of Christ; she suffered daily for Him. There are many others who have done the same thing, they put their lives on hold to express and be the Jesus all men will see. No disrespect to the martyrs, but it is often easier to die as a martyr than to live as one dead to self and alive only for Christ. It seems to me that some churches have placed an undo emphasis on the death of a martyred saint and in so doing, diminished the lives of other true and living saints. I believe this is a result of not understanding Revelation. Is the blood and death of a saint of more value than those who stood the test of time in the face of suffering and patient endurance? I don't think so!

We are in many tribulations, which John refers to as suffering, and it is because we are participating in the kingdom of God on the earth today. We have too many calling themselves believers who are just going through motions, without the relationship that's required of genuine believers to walk as His brothers and sisters of Christ. They are not interested in enduring; they have come on board for what someone told them was a promise of heaven and blessing to those who believe. Tribulation for the saints comes, because we are in the kingdom of heaven that Jesus said had come to earth when He came.

The Voice

The visions begin to unfold, and John begins describing what he's seeing, hearing, and experiencing. To set up the aura of the vision, John begins by explaining in *Revelation 1:10 (HCSB)* that, "I was in the Spirit <u>on the Lord's Day</u>." The word "Spirit" as John wrote it begins with a capital letter, which means John was referring to Holy Spirit. On this particular Lord's Day, John was operating way above the normal abilities of a man as his redeemed spirit joined with Holy Spirit in order to conduct kingdom business. Jesus came on Sunday to reveal His plan to John.

John had experienced and walked with Jesus enough to understand the importance of observing the Lord's Day. Since the First Century, Christians have been celebrating Christ and worshipping in public on Sundays. Jesus emphasized the first day of the week as the Lord's Day through His <u>resurrection</u>, <u>Pentecost</u>, and <u>Passover</u> **as they all took place on Sunday**.

Then, from behind him came this loud, alarming, piercing sound that was as loud as a trumpet. It's important to point out that John heard a loud "voice", not a trumpet. The word trumpet here is used in an allegorical or symbolic style to explain to the reader the magnitude of the voice that got his attention. John was already in the Spirit, why would the voice come from behind him instead of in front of him or above him? He was in position, ready, watching, listening, and alert, yet the voice caught him by surprise. I believe the loud voice behind him was Jesus ringing His Words into John's ears pulsing through his body as he was in a heightened state of awareness in preparation for what was about to take place. Have you ever heard someone call your name so loud that it made you jump, and you turned around to see who was speaking? This was John's response.

Brilliance

Upon hearing the startling voice John frantically turned toward the sound, and as he turned, he began to see the vision unfold before his eyes. He described what he saw in *Revelation 1:12-16a (HCSB)*, *"I turned to see whose voice it was that spoke to me. When I turned, I saw seven gold lampstands, and among the lampstands was One like the Son of Man, dressed in a long robe and with a gold sash (BYSSOS – maybe) wrapped around His chest. His head and hair were white like wool—white as snow—and His eyes like a fiery flame. His feet were like polished brass refined in a furnace, and His voice like the sound of cascading waters. He had seven stars in His right hand;"* Amazing! Can you imagine the Son of Man standing before you and the view of grandeur, the magnificence of His presence overtaking you? John described it beautifully, almost to the point that you felt as though you were there seeing exactly what he saw, feeling the magnitude of what he felt. It's breath-taking.

In this first vision, John describes a picture of Jesus, the Son of Man. He begins with seven lampstands that were made of gold and very large in stature with a grand pedestal containing oil to fuel the light coming from each of them. Each one was precious and valuable as they represented the light to the world.

In the center of the lampstands was Jesus surrounded by the seven churches. These lampstands are symbolic of the seven churches that were called to light the way of the known world. Just as Matthew said, *"You are the light of the world. A town built on a hill cannot be hidden"* (Matthew 5:14 NIV). Those who are in Christ are to be that light for the world to see. The picture I get is Jesus, by His presence, holding up the seven churches.

As John continues, he is encapsulated in the appearance of Jesus as he describes Him in His new glorified body. His attention to detail is very evident as John paints the picture using phrases like, *"His hair and head were white like wool, white as snow."* Hair like wool is a reflection of Jesus' covering over the church, and *white as [freshly fallen*, emphasis added] *snow* represents His purity. In this description, one can consider His hair was full and completely covered His head, just as a snow covers, in the purest white, everything it falls on. Then, His eyes were as flames of fire, penetrating power that pierces, and burns through anything that is not pure. Nothing is hidden from His eyes—good or bad. Though we don't know the color of the robe Jesus wore, we do know that His belt was made of gold and extended from his waist to his pectorals. His feet are described as polished, fine brass refined in a furnace. Brass is known as a pure, very defined material that when polished has a brilliant shine. The word *brass* here means *whiteness* or *brilliance*, <u>not metal</u>. It is compared to highly shined metal in appearance. John's description of Jesus' feet said that they *shined* like metal, not that they were metal. The impression presented is that Jesus' feet are hot and glowing and perhaps would burn anything they touch that is not pure, holy, or devoted. Wherever they step, things would change, and whatever they step on would never be the same.

The best comparison of the visit John experienced is found in the Book of Daniel, Chapter 10. Daniel gives us a very clear description of what John was seeing and hearing as Daniel described in detail his vision of a warring angel. *"His body was like topaz, his face like lightning, his eyes like flaming torches, his arms and legs like the gleam of burnished bronze, and his voice like the sound of a multitude"* (Daniel 10:6 NIV). When we read Daniel, we know what the voice sounded like behind John; it was the sound of a multitude of people to Daniel, and the sound of a trumpet to John, so we know why both men were overwhelmed when they had their visions. The heavenly voice has also been described as the "sound of many waters."

The body of the heavenly visitor of Daniel was described as a precious stone, topaz, which is usually yellow or pale blue in color, but can also be seen in many other colors, such as pink and purple. Understanding how a precious stone reflects light, as a prism, gives a full effect of the body of the heavenly visitor Daniel describes.

The face of the warring angel that Daniel saw had an intensity and likeness of lightening with eyes as flaming torches. Lightening is so bright and powerful that it appears frightening and overpowering at the same time, with such intensity you cannot look directly at it. The eyes of the angel were like flaming torches that light the way and reveal what is hidden in the dark.

Thinking back over the visions of both John and Daniel, we get the impression that they had similar reactions when they received their visions. *Daniel 10:7* revealed that those who were with Daniel were terrified when Daniel got the vision, but yet they saw nothing. Did they hear the voice of the heavenly visitor—it does not say? Was it the heavenly presence that created terror in them—YES, I believe it was. Daniel, describing his reaction, helps us understand the intensity of his response as he had no strength and his face turned deathly pale, and he was helpless. That means Daniel felt the blood drain from his face in fear. John had the same reaction; he fell as though he were dead. All of his nerves and muscles could no longer support him in the presence of his Lord, and he collapsed in a heap. It was not fear, as we understand fear, but the sense of the majesty and awe of God before him. Jesus spoke to him and said, "I am."

I am absolute authority, and I am the creator of all things, "I *have* the first word, and I *am* the last word spoken." Since He is Alpha and Omega, the beginning, and the end, who would be foolish enough to stand in the middle and proclaim another way? Yet, it is done every day by those who have become fools and want to go their own way.

Messengers

Along with the lampstands, John describes that he saw Jesus holding seven stars in His hand. Stars, why stars? He could have used any other words, but He chose stars. Stars are used to bring light into darkness, to shine light on our pathway. The stars Jesus is holding represent the seven pastors of the seven churches. Through John's scribing, Jesus reveals the secret of the seven stars and the seven lampstands in *Revelation 1:20* (HCSB), *"The secret of the seven stars you saw in My right hand and of the seven gold lampstands is this: The seven stars are the angels of the seven churches, and the seven lampstands are the seven churches."* A better translation of the word *aggellos* than angels is *messengers*, which better describe the intention and meaning of what Christ was portraying. Jesus charged the messengers with a great responsibility of overseeing the churches and speaking on behalf of God. These messengers, also known as preachers today, are ones carrying the Lord's messages to the church, being Christ's right-hand ministering in the churches under His majestic authority to carry out His will. This is a vision that every minister should take to heart. The symbolism of the lampstands and the stars is very relevant to us today.

Over the years, because of the failure of those who have been assigned to be the stars of Christ, the term pastor has taken on meanings that were never meant, when the title and the requirement was given by Christ. Some Pastors are now seen as charlatans, some as mockers, some as abusers of children. Some seem to be called to clean the church, to mow the church grass, and answer to a group of men who have been elected to keep the pastor under the control of the people. Sadly, because of the history of the church, since the third century, this has been for some, a very necessary condition, but from the beginning, this was not how Jesus intended for the stars, His pastors, those He held in His hand, to behave or be received.

In today's world, when people hear the term stars, no one ever thinks of Pastors, instead, they look at the ones who are called stars in Hollywood. These stars are people who pretend to be someone else, and whose ideas and words have little, if any, real value, and yet they have such impact, that one wonders how so many can be so blind and so ignorant as to believe one word of what these false stars have to say. They are pretenders. How sad, the word no longer means what was first intended.

John's description intensifies as his dialect reverts to that of a divine nature as he continues seeing through the eyes of his spirit man. In *Revelation 1:16*, John describes a sharp, doubled-edged sword coming out of His mouth, referring to Jesus. The word *sharp* refers to His approach, meaning a *swift or eager approach*. This word gives the idea of sharpness or piercing swiftly. In *Revelation 19:15*, and again in *19:21*, John refers to a "sword." The Greek word for *sword* is *romphaia*. It extends from Jesus' mouth and is able to judge the ideas and thoughts of the heart and to slay the wicked. The word used for his "sword" describes a long, heavy sword almost as tall as a man, used with both hands, and was the weapon of choice by the Thracians. Notice in Revelation 16 that there is no hand swinging the sword; it is a sword in the mouth of the Almighty. **Hebrews and Isaiah express that** *the rod of the mouth* **and the** *Word of God* **are living and effective and sharper than any sword.** In the same breath, John focuses on Jesus' face. *"His face was like the sun shining in all its brilliance."* This description refers us back to *Matthew 17:2 (HCSB)*, when Matthew wrote about Jesus' transformation, *"He was transformed in front of them, and His face shone like the sun. Even His clothes became as white as the light."* We, too often, forget the glory, splendor, and power of our Lord, and we rest in what people say—people who are clay just like us.

Authority

As John finishes the description of Jesus, Jesus sets forth who He truly is. *"I am the Living One; I was dead, and now look, I am alive forever and ever, and I hold the keys of death and Hades."* Jesus sets up the church in this finalization of His description.

He explains that He is the Living One; He was dead and now He's alive forever and will always bring hope to the church. He carries the keys of death and hell, which He gives to us to use. In the original writing, both Death and Hell are presented as <u>proper names</u> beginning with a capital letter and a definite article before them, giving credence as if they are living entities. In *Revelation 6:8 (HCSB)*, John describes a picture of horsemen called Death and another called Hades, *"And I looked, and there was a pale green horse. The horseman on it was named (the) Death, and (the) Hades was following after him. Authority was given to them over a fourth of the earth, to kill by the sword, by famine, by plague, and by the wild animals of the earth."* What an interesting way to describe two entities. Death takes all lives in judgment and Hell follows Death to collect the dead in order to judge them. Hell, or a better word Hades, collects the human souls of the dead who are damned, those who refuse Jesus, until judgment day. *Hades* is referred to as the *unseen place*. Jesus calls hell *"the Gehenna"* and the *Gehenna of fire*, which is the lake of fire. Another word used for Hades is the <u>Hebrew word *sheol*</u>, which is used two times in the Old Testament, referencing *all who die leave the earth (grave)* and *those who are damned (hell)*. There is no word in the Greek or English for *sheol*. Then, in *Revelation 20:13-15*, both entities give up the dead, and Death and Hades are thrown into the lake of fire. If you think about it, you don't throw an idea or a location into a lake; you throw an entity.

Hope

It is very interesting that Jesus would tell John that He *"holds the keys of death and Hades."* I believe Jesus was encouraging the church, providing hope. We stand in the authority of Jesus no matter what the enemy throws our way, because we have the power over death and hell as we walk in Christ. In *Matthew 16:19 (NIV)*, Jesus explains that He gives us the keys of the kingdom of heaven. Every believer has access to the keys as Jesus says, *"I will give you the keys of the kingdom of heaven; whatever you bind on earth will be bound in heaven, and whatever you loose on earth will be loosed in heaven."* This is spoken and written in *plural* and shows that this was not exclusive to one but included everyone.

This means that believers can now confirm what has been decided in heaven. <u>Heaven does not have to confirm our pronouncements, only Christ's</u>.

Prior to revealing the keys to the kingdom in *Matthew 16:18*, Jesus tells Peter that He will build His church and the gates of Hades will not overcome it *(Paraphrased)*. The word "church" appears here for <u>the first time</u>. Therefore, this authority the Lord Jesus gave to Peter, and was intended for all His disciples, was the necessary apostolic authority for the establishment of the truth in the church. When Jesus released the keys of the kingdom to Peter, He said, "You can now bind and loose." The word *loose* in our churches has been somewhat misunderstood, so it is misused. To loose is to *unbind or untie* and *to let go of*. Whatever you shall loose on earth or declare is not part of the individual anymore. <u>It is removed</u> because Christ has already forgiven the sin and the price has been paid. As it is in heaven so is it on earth. It means to dissolve, sever, break off, or break up; loose the sin of the past. *John 20:23* tells us to loose off new believers their past sins. The keys to the kingdom bring freedom in Christ, a hope to all who believe.

John's magnificent, detailed description is beyond anything he had experienced in walking with Jesus. As his vision began, he established that this vision was much bigger than anything he could have ever imagined. It was a vision of supernatural proportions with an intensity, magnitude, and powerful presence that overwhelmed him to the point he knew he was in the midst of Almighty Jesus. John knew he could not have described what he was seeing without the guidance of Holy Spirit.

JESUS IN THE MIDST OF THE EPHESUS CHURCH

CHAPTER 2

Have you ever wondered why Jesus instructed John to write to seven churches in the Book of Revelation? Why not just one church, one letter addressing all the issues at one time across the board? What we do know is that each letter represents the condition of churches in general, even today. It gave Him an opportunity to address issues that would transcend time and focus on specific problems.

As John turns his focus, unfolding before him is Jesus walking in the midst of these seven churches telling John what He is observing. He sees their condition, their problematic issues, and their future. Each church would receive a letter from

Jesus providing specific content for their needs to include instruction, correction, and edification. The letters were not written in a generic form, but followed a similar pattern, very pointed for each location, and addressed the struggles that many were facing. John began each letter by addressing it to the angel of the given city. Then, he established the author of the letter, which was Jesus. Followed by, in most instances, some praise, correction, and announcement that anyone who has ears to hear pay attention to what the Spirit says. Finally, each letter ends with an eschatological promise, a focus on what is to come.

John establishes to whom the first letter is addressed, *"To the angel of the church of Ephesus write: These are the words of him who holds the seven stars in his right hand and walks among the seven golden lampstands" (Revelation 2:1 NIV)*. His first focus was the church in Ephesus. Ephesus was the closest city of the seven to Patmos. It had been John's place of operation, since the seven-year Jewish War where the Jews fought the Romans in 66-73 (AD). This war resulted in the destruction of Jerusalem, which took place 25 years prior to John's encounter. We never hear about this war; we only talk about the results of Jews being thrown out.

According to Josephus in the book entitled, "The War of the Jews," the view of Judea was a depressing site after the war. A lot like that of southern Florida when hurricane Andrew leveled Homestead years ago. And more recently, the devastation of Marianna, Mexico Beach, and Panama City, Florida from the destruction of hurricane Michael. They were all places that experienced destruction, so devastating, that one could only remember and reminisce of what once was. In Judea, the places that previously flourished with trees and beautiful gardens were now desolate in every way. Any foreigner who had formerly seen Judea and the most beautiful suburbs of the city, now saw it as a desert, no longer recognizable. The war had removed all the signs of beauty and left nothing but waste. The Roman legions had cut every beautiful tree, trampled every garden or anything that had beauty, and destroyed the walls. All was desolate.

Emperor Titus actually led his men against Jerusalem and gave thanks to God for their success, when he acclaimed and encouraged his soldiers. They burned the gates of the temple and piled up bodies from both sides resulting in the stench of rotting flesh everywhere.

Daniel had actually prophesied 606 years prior, that the Romans, "in <u>half a week</u> would cause the sacrifice and oblation *(the thing offered to God)* to cease" *(Daniel 9:27, Paraphrased).* Vespasian entered this war about <u>three and a half years</u> from the month of February 66 A.D. to the end of this time. <u>The year</u> closely confirms the duration of the war; four years <u>before the war</u> began was about seven years five months before the destruction of Jerusalem. **They called it the <u>Tribulation</u>.**

Church of Ephesus

The church in Ephesus was established in 55 A.D., and now in 95 A.D., it is 40 years old. **The church was located in the city of <u>Ephesus</u>,** which was the capitol of the province, and due to its location was the most important from the start. It was situated on an isthmus and everyone from the east or the west had to go through Ephesus, which housed a 40-foot statue of Artemis/Dianna to worship.

Warning

Jesus began describing to John what He was observing in regard to the church at Ephesus. As He started the letter, He explained to them that He knew where they were, what they were going through, and how well they handled what was before them. He let them know that He understood. He saw the work they were doing, the labor intensity of their endurance, and the stance they made against evil. I am fascinated by the word Jesus chose in *Revelation 2:2 (HCSB)* when he said, "you cannot tolerate evil." The King James Version says *evil*, the New International Version says *wicked*, and the Amplified Version says *base ones*. The Greek word is *kakos* and is the word used to refer to *manure, and also someone who appears worthless and cowardly*. Here Jesus is describing those who called themselves apostles and were not, those who were good for nothing in regard to what they should be. A lazy student of the word, a soldier who runs from the battle, and a disgraceful church member are all described as *kakos*. <u>It does not mean</u> vicious, wicked, or evil exactly, <u>but it can lean toward</u> those descriptions. If *Revelation 2:2* had been translated literally, it would say... "you cannot tolerate crap/manure, or someone who appears worthless or cowardly."

The church of Ephesus had endured and tolerated many things because of Christ. They endured those who presented themselves as something more than they were, and yet, the church continued to strive and stay true to the gospel they had at first.

Then, Jesus threw out the curve ball, and presented the current condition of the church. He explained that their love was "still alive," but dissipating. Their passion and enthusiasm for Him had fallen away and was still falling away. The love was NOT gone, but the first love, the excited love, the new love, the love with passion and desire was gone. Jesus was alarmed, because He knew that love with passion should grow stronger the more they know Christ, and the more they make His words their words. Jesus said in *John 14:15 (HCSB)*, "If you love Me, you will keep My commands."

And again, in *John 14:23 (HCSB)*, Jesus answered, "If anyone loves Me, he will keep My word. My Father will love him, and <u>We</u> will come to him and make <u>Our</u> home with him." Jesus did not see this love happening in the church in Ephesus. When passion and enthusiasm decline, genuine love declines. The next step is a downhill spiral in the relationship with Christ, until the relationship with Him declines even more and finally in totality. Jesus said that only the FIRST decline had taken place. They were being warned to stop before it went any further, because if they did not stop, the decline would continue. They were losing their passion.

A degree of passion is necessary in every relationship because it makes us want to keep the relationship alive and ongoing. When we pray for someone <u>without passion</u>, the prayer is almost subjective and perfunctory. But when we pray with passion, we demand, interject, call, dig, and we plant *what we want for them*—it is a totally different prayer with totally different results. So, how do you get passion back? How do you stir up a passion for a love that was beyond anything you ever experienced? What does it take to ignite that spark once again? These may have been questions the people in the church of Ephesus were asking. Some may have even had a desire for it but did not know what to do to get it back. Jesus, in His all-knowing, understood their questions, their desires, and the longings that they had to go back to their first love. This is very evident in his instruction to them as He told them to go back, remember, and do again what they did at first. I can just imagine His conversation. *"Go ahead, think back to the first time we met. Do you remember the love and passion that you had for Me? Go back and remember what you did in the beginning. Rekindle that flame before it goes out"* (Revelation 2:5, Paraphrased). He lovingly told them what they needed to do. *Luke 3:8* encourages us to do again the things that are worthy of repentance. If married couples

<u>would do this, we would see fewer divorces.</u> Repentance without change is pretense, and pretense is a lie to God and us.

In today's society, the word *repent* carries with it a stigma. When we hear that word, we immediately think that we have failed, or we have been doing something terribly wrong intentionally. There are times when we are called to repentance when we have buried something deep in our heart, and God wants to deliver us from that burden, hurt, or whatever the case may be. These times of repentance are very sweet, because this is when Jesus comes in to heal those areas and help us move closer to Him to rekindle that first love. It stirs in us a passion, because we realize that He loves us enough to pull out of us what is not of Him.

Jesus warned the church of Ephesus, because there was still time to repent, but time was running out. He told them, "If you do not actually repent, there will be judgment." The verb used here for *repent* is *aorist* and is used to express *actuality*. He says if you do not actually repent, change your mind and your direction, I will remove your lampstand. There is now no church of any denomination in Ephesus—it is apparent that they did not heed the warning of Jesus.

Several years ago, Turkish Prime Minister Erdogan put the world on notice that he was God. He was calling for the antichrist to appear and announced plans to form a new Islamic Union led by Turkey. He established his desire to reinstate the Turkish ruled Ottoman Empire. The Turkish Prime Minister, of course, was not God. He just tried to convince others that he was. This is a prime example of what the church of Ephesus was facing. In 2 *Thessalonians 2:3-4, we are warned to not be deceived in any way, for that day of the coming of our Lord Jesus Christ will not come until the rebellion occurs and the man of lawlessness is revealed, the man doomed to destruction. He will oppose and will exalt himself over everything that is called God or is worshipped, so that he sets himself up in God's temple proclaiming himself to be God (Paraphrased).* Jesus warned the church of Ephesus, but they just chose not to listen.

Today, there is not one church standing in this entire area of Turkey that John is writing about. The light has been removed, Ephesus is gone – Philadelphia is gone and all the others are but a memory written on paper. The only thing left in Turkey is the darkness, and it is already raining darkness there.

Nicolaitans

Jesus admonished those in Ephesus, when He commended them for hating the Nicolaitans, which Jesus also hated. The Nicolaitans were an early Gnostic group that operated and functioned as superior to everyone around them claiming to have knowledge that others did not have. The word Nicolaitans comes from the word *Nicholas*, which means *conqueror*, and the term Gnostic means *claiming to have esoteric knowledge*, which is knowledge others do not have. The idea behind this word focuses on a small number of people with special knowledge who can understand what is taking place or what is pertinent or important.

In *Revelation 2:6*, when John references the group of people known as the Nicolaitans, he was describing a group that conducted themselves in ways that Jesus hated. The term Nicolaitans refers to a *conqueror of the people*. The Nicolaitans still exit today.

Balaam, the prophet that was saved from the avenging angel by his donkey was considered a conqueror of the people as referenced in Numbers 23. This term is found elsewhere to reveal the separation of the body members of the church with the leadership, referring to the people as the laity, and the leadership as the presbytery. This is what GOD says He HATES. The Roman Catholic Church and even some denominational churches practice this in order to subjugate the people. The term they use for priests is "father" and Jesus said do not call any man father, master, or reverend in the sense of your spiritual leader. They use the term *Monsignor*, which means *my lord*, when addressing regional priests. The Roman Catholic Church refers to the pope as the Vicar of Christ. The word *vicar* means *in place of*. If God hated the conqueror attitude and behavior when Jesus told John to write this, He hates it now.

The term *Vicar of Christ* is not an innocent term. The original meaning comes from Latin, and it means *a substitute or in place of another,* and in this case the other is Christ. The current pope is doing everything within his power to align and unite Islam with Catholicism similar to what President Obama was doing with Persia, or Iran, the mortal enemy of Israel and Christianity.

Roman Catholic Church Decline

The Roman Catholic Church continued to decline in their practice as they exalted themselves above everything. In 300 A.D., the Roman Catholic Church began praying *for* and *to* the dead, a pagan practice and began making the sign of the cross which is actually a "T" used by pagans to remember Tammuz. In 375 A.D., they began another pagan practice of worshiping dead saints. In 394 A.D., Mass was first instituted, and 200 years later all Masses were conducted in Latin, which few people, if any, understood. Then, in 431 A.D., the Roman Catholic Church began the veneration and worship of Mary, and prayers were being directed to Mary in 600 A.D.

Over the years, the Catholic Church has worked hard on establishing themselves as a "higher power" church. The medieval Catholic Church sold indulgences, where men thought they could operate as God by granting other men amnesty from punishment for sin in this life and the one hereafter. Pope John Paul II announced that Catholic penitents would receive indulgences for such good deeds as quitting smoking, abstaining from alcohol, or performing a charitable act. The practice of indulgences drove Martin Luther to rebel and write his 95 *Thesis*, which he nailed to the church door in Whittenburg, Germany. This began the reformation in the Sixteenth Century. Indulgences these days are granted to those who carry out certain tasks such as climbing the Sacred Steps in Rome, which is a weeklong event held in July of each year. Mindful of the faithful who cannot afford to fly to Brazil, the Vatican's Sacred Apostolic Penitentiary, a court which handles the forgiveness of sins, has also extended the privilege to those following the "rites and pious exercises" of the event on television, radio and through social media. "That includes indulgences for following Twitter," said a source at the Penitentiary, referring to Pope Francis' Twitter account, which has gathered over seven million followers.

Then, in 1998, Pope John Paul II announced that he made arrangements with heavenly powers to let people out of purgatory early when they die, if they would perform good deeds. Pope Gregory, nothing more than a mere mortal man, is credited with the start of purgatory in 1170 A.D., and every pope since then has continued this "make believe" location to keep the followers in subjection, based upon fear. Purgatory began in the minds of the pagan worshippers, long before Christ. I learned, just as Luther did, salvation is a gift and NOT something we perform works to obtain. Why continue something that is not true, never found in the Bible and never spoken by the apostles? The reason is because it subjugates and controls the people; it conquers the people. **Purgatory, according to the Roman Catholic Church website is an**

intermediate state after physical death in which those destined for heaven undergo purification to achieve enough holiness to enter heaven. I always thought that we did that here on earth with help from Holy Spirit. What happened to Jesus and salvation being the only way to the Father and heaven? John said it best in *John 14:6 (NIV), "Jesus answered, 'I am the way and the truth and the life. No one comes to the Father except through me.'"*

All the actions of the Catholic Church mimic the behaviors of the Nicolaitan church which is still in operation today commanding the lives of over one billion people. The message the Nicolaitan's proclaimed, as well as that of the Catholic Church, were very different from those who follow Christ. Dr. M.R. DeHaan, a prophetic Bible teacher was quoted saying, "To come to Christ costs nothing, to follow Christ costs something, but to serve Christ costs everything." *Matthew 10:39 (HCSB)* tells us the same thing, *"Anyone finding his life will lose it, and anyone losing his life, because of Me will find it."* The message of Christ tells us to lay down our life for Him, and He will build us up.

To gain better understanding of what Jesus was telling the church in Ephesus, let's breakdown the word Nicolaitans further. *Niko* means *to overthrow*. *Laos* means the *laity* or *any who are not Clergy*. It seems that in the early church years, two problems remained causing consistent problems within the ranks, Judaism and Nicolaitanism.

Historically, we see the establishment of bishops, archbishops, cardinals, and popes, and at one point there were two popes in two different locations. This practice of ecclesiasticism is not scriptural at all. It causes the local church to become enslaved by one man or a small group of men, whose spiritual life or lack of it, is what determines the spiritual success of the church. Ecclesiasticism was carried over into the reformation with John Calvin, who left the Roman Catholic Church in the reformation, but took most of the Ecclesiastical practices with him, except the pope and the idea of a pope. Too often, men who start out holy end up being unholy after they take office, because they are given power too early and become in their own minds, absolute. It does not matter whether they come from independent or denominational churches. This causes the people, "who are not clergy", to look at human beings for solutions to their problems, instead of Holy Spirit who brings and guides you into all truth. *For He does not speak on His own, but He speaks whatever He hears the Father saying (John 16:13, Paraphrased).*

Nicolaitanism is synonymous with modern day ecclesiasticism, which is the practice Jesus said, "I hate". Today, it is a curse running without any interference. When a mere man or small group of men control the entire training and nurturing of other people, they are in a position to dominate the church, however, not everyone bought into the Nicolaitanism practices or the Roman Catholic Church.

An Englishman named John Wycliffe was well known throughout Europe for his opposition to the organized Roman Catholic Church and was condemned for translating the first Bible from Latin to English. He was the one given credit for the reformation. The Pope was so infuriated by his teachings and his translation of the Bible that 44 years after Wycliffe died, he ordered the bones dug up, crushed, and scattered into the river.

DR. DAVID DEL VECCHIO with DIANE BRILEY

THE AMERICAN CHURCH

CHAPTER 3

Jesus counseled the church at Ephesus to do four things: <u>remember</u> how far you have fallen, <u>repent</u> and <u>return</u> to how you behaved when you first found Christ, and <u>do again</u> what you did when you knew who He was in you. In the Gospel of *John 14:15 (HCSB)*, Jesus explained, "If you love me, you will keep My commands." Throughout the history of the church, we can see the battle the Ephesian church faced was real. They were constantly bombarded with those who tried to exalt themselves above Jesus, yet they stayed true to who they really were. Their downfall was that they lost their first love.

This is much like the churches in America today. I can only imagine what Jesus would say if He were to write a letter addressed to us. That's a very sobering thought. Would we fall into the category of the Ephesian church?

Would He tell us to go back and find our first love? Would He plead with us to love Him like we did at first, with total abandon? He has provided everything we need to live a life unashamed, abandoned in love with Him. *He has given us the power to overcome the world, if we are born of God and believe that Jesus is the Son of God (1 John 5:4-5, Paraphrased).* Or would He be angry with us as He was with the Hebrew Christians, because of their laziness? *Hebrews 5:11-12 explains that the Hebrew Christians had become too lazy to understand, so they needed someone to teach them the basic principles of God's revelation again. They should have been able to receive solid food, but instead they still needed milk, because they became stagnate in their walk.*

James, the pastor of the first or early church recognized this within his church. He told his congregation *not to deceive themselves and merely listen to the Word, <u>but do what it says</u> (James 1:22, Paraphrased).* The word for *listen* is *akroates,* which means *listen without practicing.* The word for *do* is *poiet'es,* which means *perform.* James understood and he wanted his people to understand that you must live what you learn. This is what the church in Ephesus needed to remember. They needed to go back to their first love.

Can you imagine trying to live a Christian life without the Bible? We have the ability to review and review and review the Word of God over and over again to gain the concepts and principles of the Christian life, because of the written Word. But the Ephesian church did not, yet they were expected to live a Christian life. Christians today have no excuse for allowing the world to remain in us. We have no excuse for responding with the words of the world, instead of the Words of Christ. We are even given the "how to" in *Colossians 3:5-8 (NIV)* where it states, *"Put to death whatever belongs to your earthly nature: sexual immorality, impurity, lust, evil desires and greed, which is idolatry. Because of these, the wrath of God is coming. You used to walk in these ways, in the life you once lived. But now you must also rid yourselves of all such things as these: anger, rage, malice, slander, and filthy language from your lips."*

In America, we see every day the results of people living without God as their Leader, Savior, Deliverer, and Conqueror, when we look at the issues of same sex marriage and abortion. Several years ago, a major denomination (Methodist) in five major US cities put both a Bible and a Koran on the pew next to each other and the pastors taught on blending the two religions into one called Christlam—<u>an abomination</u> truly has come to America. The Supreme Court even voted for same sex marriage, which put this nation under judgment. The Lord has held off from His judgment for the evil this country has committed by murdering over 50 million babies, but He will remove His blessing and send His curse unless the church wakes up and prays.

America is still a Christian nation, however, it has just lost its first love and surrendered to weakness and sinful behavior. Some of the foundational Christian truths are being exchanged for a lie, just as Paul said in *Romans 1:25-27 (NIV),* *"They exchanged the truth about God for a lie, and worshiped and served created things rather than the Creator—who is forever praised. Amen. Because of this, God gave them over to shameful lusts. Even their women exchanged natural sexual relations for unnatural ones. In the same way, the men also abandoned natural relations with women and were inflamed with lust for one another. Men committed shameful acts with other men, and received in themselves the due penalty for their error."* It is important not to allow anyone to pull the wool over our lives or lead us astray from the truth. Due to our own ignorance and desire to include others, we think all believers are as we are – <u>they are not</u>.

Here is what I mean by that. The Roman Catholic Church today meets every requirement to be called the modern day Nicolaitans. From 2007 to 2015, the percentage of Christians or Protestants has declined 8% or a drop of five million adults a year. The Muslim religion has increased by more than that during this time. The single greatest drop was in the Roman

Catholic Church, which was 3% of the total American population and another 3% drop out of South America.

One reason for this is the new pope's endorsement of *Theistic Evolution* and his endorsement of the *Global Warming* belief, which leaves God out, and is a liberal <u>left wing only view</u>. This pope is also committed to a social gospel, nothing like the Catholics were used to before his entry into this office. So, many Catholics are looking for something different, something that does not bend.

The *Theistic Evolution* is a range of view about how evolution relates to religious beliefs. Since evolution is a lie, why would anyone who claims Christ as Lord believe any of it, even for a second, and then try to rationalize the word of the Lord with it? Throughout church history, evolution has evolved, building upon it lie upon lie. The Protestant denominations are not exempt. The greatest drop in the Protestant arena is at the liberal end. Episcopalians now have a homosexual state bishop, and some factions of the Methodists, Lutherans, and

Presbyterians <u>openly accept</u> the lifestyles of homosexuals. Not everyone who calls himself or herself a Christian truly are. Some rationalize their way through to believe what they want to believe, to justify their actions. In some cases, the lie is built upon the fear of offense, such as the homosexual movement. To keep from offending someone, the church has accepted the lifestyle instead of simply loving the person but rejecting the lifestyle. There is a difference.

<u>Liberalism fosters sin without consequences</u>. It is emotion without knowledge. Liberalism, which is way left of conservative thinking will justify abortion, euthanasia, suicide, and non-traditional marriage. Any group advocating homosexual marriage or abortion is a liberal group, because in their hearts they say there is no God, no matter what they say publicly. They say anyone who operates in faith is mentally defective. They also refuse to acknowledge the evil of Islam, because they think they can win the hearts of Muslims by social awareness. These people are woefully ignorant and dangerous

to the rest who know better. Islam is a religion of hate, separation, Nicolaitanism and murder.

These liberal denominations are ordaining homosexual ministers, performing gay/lesbian marriages, and have so watered down the word they have no Gospel left in them whatsoever. Now, what they have is a social gospel, and I believe in our lifetime we will see them come to an end. It is very evident that Revelation is now happening before our eyes, and we need to be awakened.

DR. DAVID DEL VECCHIO with DIANE BRILEY

SMYRNA: A CHURCH OF SPIRITUAL RICHES

CHAPTER 4

The visions kept coming at John as he turned to see the next church that Jesus was addressing. When Jesus began to write to the church in Smyrna, His approach was quite different from that of Ephesus. He did not warn them or rebuke them. Instead, He simply told them He knew their affliction and poverty, and the tribulation they had endured. Jesus let them know that He understood where they were. Their tribulation was severe and unimaginable.

The poverty they endured was a way of life for all Christians because they were not allowed to work, sell, or be involved in

most methods of sustaining life. And their affliction was their common cross. Jesus said, "I know your afflictions."

We are seeing the beginning of what the Smyrna believers faced take place in the world we currently live in with the pandemic of COVID and the variants running rampant. We are seeing in parts of our nation that the vaccine for COVID is being mandatory to work, sell, or be involved in most methods of sustaining life. <u>They are even talking about a chip</u> to place under the skin of your hand or on your head to prove that you had the COVID vaccine. I wonder how the world will use the vaccination mandates to enforce the new cults upon those who refuse the mandates, which have ultimately been designated for political control, and the end of public Christianity.

Smyrna

Smyrna was a trade city built of guilds. The tradesmen formed unions, much the same as what was displayed in the 30's, 40's and 50's in America, but the trades and unions of Smyrna were even worse. If one did not participate in the trades which was predominately a cult religion, he was out. It is possible that the businesses of Christians were not successful, because they were blackballed, making most work unavailable to them causing them to live in poverty, because of the persecution. The guilds would make sure that Christians did not get any work, except for what men in the guild refused to do.

History of Smyrna

The church at Smyrna was located 35 miles east of Ephesus. It was the nicest city of cities and considered the pride of Asia. Emperor worship began here, and Christians suffered greatly, because they would not worship Caesar. Polycarp, who became the bishop over the region, was martyred here in 151 A.D., because he refused to call Caesar lord. **Notice that Jesus does not offer the church at Smyrna a rebuke or a commendation as he does Ephesus.**

Those who proclaimed to be Jews and were not, were considered and mentioned here by Jesus, in fact, He calls them satanists—those who worship Satan, based upon their behavior. They did not think they were satanists, they simply thought they were protecting the cause of Judaism, but that is not what God thought. This is a written lesson telling us to be careful how we judge what we do not know.

This church age saw a number of the ten periods of testing under emperor persecution. From 34 to 60 A.D., the Jews were in some revolt or another against Rome. In 64 A.D., the persecution of Christians began in earnest. The Coliseum was built from 71-80 A.D., and, of course, was the venue of horror for the Christians. Nero [54-68 A.D.] beheaded Paul, crucified Peter, and in 68 A.D. committed suicide. In 70 A.D., Jerusalem was destroyed. Domitian exiles John who was now writing this for Jesus as His amanuensis. Trajan rules from 98 to 116 A.D. and burned Christians at the stake. Hadrian rules from Rome 117-138 A.D. and built the famous wall between England and Scotland. He also started the postal system. The Jews revolt against Rome under the leadership of bar Kokhba, which lasted <u>seven years</u> from 122-135 A.D., and we see the final dispersal of the Jews to other parts of the world. Marcus Aurelius ruled from

151 to 180 A.D. and killed Justin Martyr. Severus II converted the government into a military monarchy, after which we have Maximinius, Decius, Valerian, Aurelian, and then, the worst persecutor of all the Christians, Diocletian. Diocletian was considered to be the worst emperor in Rome's history. He tried to eliminate the Bible from off the face of the earth and had public confiscations and burnings of any sacred scriptures.

Faith and Works

As Jesus was addressing the Smyrna church, He did not stop at poverty and affliction, He went further to help them see they were rich. He didn't leave them in their poverty thinking. The phrase "Yet you are rich," which is inserted parenthetically, meaning there are spiritual riches that belong to them. There is a divine principle at work here that supersedes a person's economic condition. The cause of their suffering is laid at the feet of the Jews, who are from the synagogue of Satan. These are the ones who claim to be Jews, but Jesus said are not Jews.

Have you ever felt as though you were not doing enough for the Kingdom, feeling as though you need to do more, pray more, read your Bible more? Though all these things are good, and definitely encouraged, they can become a stumbling block, if used to try to earn your salvation. Those who claimed to be Jews, but were not, tried to earn their way through works by practicing two basic heresies that are still with us today. These heresies add to the saving grace of Jesus by focusing on works instead of grace that are needed for salvation. That is not only heresy, but also sin, because it removes faith, and replaces it with works to add to what Jesus did. It is by grace through faith, Paul writes in Romans, <u>not faith and works</u>.

The Jews, in trying to live by the letter of the law, kept adding rituals, such as keeping the Sabbath, what foods they were allowed to eat, and being legalistic with certain rites and ceremonies. Recall why we keep the first day of the week. Jesus said everyday was holy unto the Lord. Remember during Passover, Jesus rose from the dead on the first day of the week, and during Pentecost, He gave His Spirit to those in the upper room on Sunday, the first day of the week. In attempting to live by way of the law, the Jews taught that one should refrain from partaking of certain foods, even though Jesus said that all food was good for us to eat *(Matthew 15:10-11.*

Over the centuries, the Jews said we must keep certain rites and ceremonies, yet for almost 3000 years Judaizers have not been able to change the church. The church resisted them, however, over the years they have crept in, and through ignorance about Jesus, they have given us foolishness in place of faith. They were indeed Jews by birth and religion as opposed to Gentiles and pagans, but Jesus did not consider them Jews, by his condemning verdict.

In *Romans 2:28-29 (HCSB)*, Paul makes the same distinction as John does, *"For a person is not a Jew who is one outwardly, and (true) circumcision is not something visible in the flesh. On the contrary, a person is a Jew who is one inwardly, and circumcision is of the heart – by the Spirit, not the letter. That man's praise is not from men but from God."* In Acts, we read how the Jews accused and persecuted the Christians, so we see three different writers, Jesus, Luke, and Paul, say the same thing about those who are born into Judaism and those who have become a part of Satan's synagogue. Jesus calls them the synagogue of Satan, not the building, but those individuals who gathered and blasphemed, and persecuted the Christians. They were doing Satan's work, thinking they were in defense of Judaism.

<u>Unlike any other belief</u>, Christianity is the only one where believers can take it with them when they go from this life. We can send it ahead. Matthew explains it in *Matthew 6:19-20 (NIV)*, *"Do not store up for yourselves treasures on earth, where moths and vermin destroy, and where thieves break in and steal. But store up for yourselves treasures in heaven, where moths and vermin do not destroy, and where thieves do not break in and steal."*

As John continues to scribe for Jesus in the letter to the church of Smyrna, he describes some of the things they will face. He displays a church going through martyrdom. He does not censure the church but lays everything out for them. Some key words that automatically jump out are not very pleasant ones. I think if some of us had received this letter, our hearts would drop to our stomach. **None of us like to suffer, be imprisoned, be tested or persecuted, but those are the things Jesus said was coming to those who were part of the church of Smyrna.** However, Jesus did not stop there, he encouraged them to not be afraid, be faithful and there would be a reward for them, a victor's crown. The Greek word for crown is *stephanos*, which can mean *crown of victory for winning the games*. The victor's crown that we picture is not always made of metal with jewels on it, as we have so often pictured, but a narrow cord or thread worn on the brow; a number of them could be worn at the same time. Often, they were made of woven ivy, oak, myrtle, olive leaves, flowers or beaten gold. The woven vines of thorns placed upon Jesus' head was similar to what the Roman soldiers were used to seeing on kings, emperors and victors, a literal crown of achievement as king of the Jews, even though it was placed there to mock Him.

Jesus tells the church that He is aware of everything that is happening and will happen, and it's all part of His plan. No matter what happens, <u>do not stop</u> holding on to Christ, even to the point of death. That is very easy to say, but not so easy to do, especially when demented satanic inspired minds have ulterior motives, based upon hate against you. Much like when the Jews accused Christians of a lot of things that they were not guilty of as their property was confiscated, and they were left homeless, destitute, jailed, and tortured. This is merely an example by the devil for what's about to come against Christianity when the world takes on the mark of the beast and believers refuse to accept it.

When John scribed the words in *Revelation 2:10* (NIV) as, *"put in prison to test you or try you, and you will suffer persecution for ten days."* He did not mean they were there to be put on trial by the pagan courts for ten days. He was referencing a form of <u>symbolical language</u>. What John wrote in this verse was written in the passive voice, which means God is the agent of their test, a trial of faith. **The test does not mean to *tempt*, but to place on**

trial by suffering. As you may well know, trials are not the easiest thing to walk through. Even with a faith that is steadfast, trials can be challenging, yet rewarding. Jesus knew this, He knew that there would be those who would walk through their trials with fear, so strong that they would be tempted to renounce Christ. He helped them see that He truly understood where they were and provided a hope for them.

Those who were not born again could not understand Jesus' hope, when He talked about the second death in *Revelation 2:11*, but those who had ears to hear completely understood what Jesus was referring too, His ultimate return. This same principal applies to you and me as well. If we do not cave in to the trials of this life, we have a hope and a promise that He will see us through them, and we will be victorious. We just have to keep our focus on Him instead of our trials or circumstances.

PERGAMUM: FAITHFUL YET WORLDLY

CHAPTER 5

Pergamum

In continuing with John's role as scribe, he begins the next letter to the church of Pergamum. This vision unfolds as John is instructed to write to the angel of the church in Pergamum. Very interesting that John refers to the author of this letter as, "Him who has the sharp, double-edged sword." As previously mentioned, the sharp sword with two edges is symbolic of God's omnipotent power as it devours His enemies. How do you see Jesus? Do you envision Him as strong and mighty, with omnipotent power, or do you see Him still in a manger, lying on hay wrapped in swaddling clothes as is portrayed at Christmas time? How about still on the cross instead of risen again? This verse in *Revelation 2:12* describes a very different image of Jesus, who is strong and mighty and wields a great sword that swings from His mouth and His words cut and change worlds. The Lamb has become the Lion.

The Seat of Satan

Genesis records that after the flood of Noah, one of his sons, Ham, had born a son named Cush. Cush married a woman named Semiramis, who bore a son named Nimrod. Nimrod married his own mother, after Cush's death, and became a powerful King over a place called Babylon. Babylon was once the seat or place of Satan, which was the place where Nimrod ruled with his mother, who was also his wife, Semiramis. When the glory of Babylon began to decline, Satan looked for another place to take up his seat, and Pergamum had become so active and so evil, it became his home.

Pergamum had a cluster of famous pagan temples, including one to Zeus, the king of all mythological gods, and other false gods with other temples devoted to Minerva, Apollo, Venus, and Bacchus. Out of the seven cities to which Jesus was writing, Pergamum was the worst pagan city. This is why Jesus said this was where Satan had his throne.

In 29 B.C., a temple had been built to honor the Emperor Augustus who was considered divine. In that same year, another temple had been built to honor the goddess Roma, who was served by a very large contingent of priests. The city was full of evil. Set within its borders was the cult of Aesculapius, whose symbol was the serpent and was called the god of Pergamum. **Aesculapius is the sign used by physicians and drugstores as the symbol of medicine that is still used today.**

John continues to scribe what Jesus is saying to the church of Pergamum as the church was condemned because some were holding to the teaching of Balaam and the Nicolaitans. The teaching included eating meat sacrificed to idols and to the commitment of sexual immorality.

Numbers, chapters 22 through 31, displays Balaam's account. Balak, the king of Moab, hired Balaam to use his prophetic gift to pronounce declarations and prophesy against Israel, because Balak was afraid of Israel, but every time Balaam tried, he ended up blessing Israel instead. Can you imagine trying to get words to come out of your mouth to speak against someone and instead, the words that actually came out were blessings, encouragement, nice, sweet words? Every time Balaam opened his mouth, the words he formed in his mind were not what came out of his mouth. He tried his best to curse Israel, so he could get the money Balak promised him, but nothing was working. The harder he tried; the more blessed Israel became.

Finally, in desperation, he told Balak to entice Israel to intermarry the women of Moab. This became the trap that destroyed many of them. At Balaam's suggestion and with his encouragement, which was received, because he was well respected for his prophetic gift, Israel intermarried with Moab against God's previous command and polluted the entire nation. This is what Jesus references in *Revelation 2:14*.

It has always amazed me how those who sin like to gather around others who have similar hearts, even if the others do not practice the specific sins themselves. It's as if they know the others would sin, but something holds them back and often it's the fear of exposure and not the fear of God. It becomes easier to sin when those around us are sinning and doing what we once did. Some in the church at Pergamum were giving into temptation and encouraging others to do the same thing. They were going back to the practice they had of eating food dedicated to idols, which was previously how they worshipped. They intermixed sex with the temple prostitutes into their practice of worship, which also provided a means for which they gave money or offerings to the temple priests. They also believed like the Nicolaitans.

As Jesus continued with the letter to the church of Pergamum, He continued to disclose those things of which He was not pleased. *Revelation 2:14 (HCSB)* states, *"But I have a few things against you. You have some there who hold to the teachings of Balaam, who taught Balak to place a stumbling block in front of the Israelites: to eat meat sacrificed to idols and to commit sexual immorality."* The word stumbling block is much better than the word enticed, but it still lacks the strength of the word that was originally written, which means TRAP. In *Romans 9:33*, Paul uses the same word when he says, "a stumbling stone" and "rock of offense." *"As it is written, behold, I lay in Zion a stumbling stone and rock of offense: and whosoever believeth on Him shall not be ashamed" (Romans 9:33 KJV).* A person can stumble, and even fall without being killed, but when a person is caught in a trap that causes death, that person will indeed die. Balaam showed king Balak how to set a trap of death for Israel. The word for trap is *skandalon*, and it refers <u>more to</u> the *bait and the trigger* of the trap than the *trap itself. Skandalon* always denotes an enticement to <u>a specific conduct</u>, which can ruin the person in question. It always takes the right bait to entice or lure the creature that you want to trap. But without the correct trigger, one that springs the trap every time, you will not catch the creature.

The Pergamum church was faithful to Christ's name and maintained their faith in God, **but they did not remain separate**

from the world and blended in with the world in their worship, which now included paganism. We can definitely see that America is much like them.

Have you ever overcome a sin and you felt drawn to others who struggle with the same sin that you overcame? Have you ever placed yourself back in the sinful environment thinking that you were strong enough to stand your ground and not give in to the sin, and the next thing you know you are in the midst of the act of the sin? Many people believe that they can do this. We see it mostly with those who have had addictions to drugs or alcohol. Yet, when they get around those who are still using, the overcomers find themselves giving in to the temptation, reverting back to the state of sinfulness again. This was the church of Pergamum.

Their intensions were honorable, but their actions were detrimental. Jesus saw what they were doing and compelled the church of Pergamum to repent, because judgment was coming, and it was coming quickly.

Constantinople and the Church

To understand the effects the Nicolaitans had on the church, it's important to look at history. According to the historical records, Constantine, and Marcus Aurelius Valerius Maxentius both fought over the throne after the death of Galerius, who was Max's father-in-law and the emperor. Constantine killed Max in the battle of Milvian Bridge in 312 A.D. in Italy. Prior to the battle, Constantine saw a vision of a cross in the sky, and heard a voice tell him, "*In hoc signo vinces,*" which is Latin for *"In this sign conquer."* He had this sign painted on the shields, which were taken into battle by every soldier. He believed God spoke to him telling him if he would accept and embrace Christianity, he would conquer his enemies. So, Constantine based his foundation for Christianity on winning a war, instead of basing it on the principles of the Christian faith. This was very evident in 323 A.D. when Constantine taught his soldiers to *respect the day of the sun,* known as *Sol Invictus.* This was celebrated as the birthday of the sun on December 25th, the same day that was established as Christ's birthday.

When we examine Constantine's life, we see his concept of Christianity as extremely flawed and perhaps had no personal relationship with Christ at all. He became emperor of the western world during the reign of Licinius, emperor of the eastern world. He defeated Licinius in battle, took control of the reunited empire, and founded the city of Constantinople on the site of Byzantium in 324 A.D. Byzantium became the name of the Eastern Roman Empire, the half that was predominately Greek speaking during the Middle Ages. Constantinople, in 330 A.D., boasted a population over a million and by the 13th Century had a recorded 5 million people living in that city. The city eventually fell to the Muslims and became known, as it is today, Istanbul, Turkey.

When Constantine became emperor, he became ruler of the known world. There was no higher authority on earth. He also became the protector of Christianity and issued laws to protect the faith. His government provided money to open and operate the churches and many temples that had previously been pagan, became places of worship for the state sponsored Christian churches. We can already see that is a serious problem. Some of the idols left in the temples were redesigned to appear as a saint and not an idol. To please Constantine, the leadership, owing him allegiance, adopted, and practiced pagan rituals and ideas. One of the rituals that was practiced was the sponsorship of the *'sunrise service'*, because he also worshipped the sun god, *Sol Invictus*. It has now become a common practice among some Christian churches, and all Roman Catholic churches to host a Sunrise Service. The church never engaged in this practice for the first three hundred years of its existence. As is true to life, *one compromise always leads to another* and what started out as a blessing, became a curse that continues today. Let me give you an example.

In the late 17th century, the Puritans, who came to America, believed, and decided that only adults with personal experience of conversion were eligible to full membership; however, it was the belief that the children shared in the covenant of their parents, and therefore, should be admitted to all the privileges of the church except the Lord's Supper. The question arose (c.1650) whether this privilege should be extended to the children of these children, even though the parents of the second generation may not have confessed any experience that brought them into full communion. It was proposed (1657) and adopted (1662) by a church synod that the privileges should be extended. Thus, the measure to which the nickname *Half-Way Covenant* became attached, as a result that is with us today. Those who embraced and accepted the Half-Way Covenant will not see heaven. Have you ever heard the old saying, "Getting to heaven on the shirt-tale of your parents?" This is where that concept originated. People thought they could get to heaven based on the actions and beliefs of their grandparents, moms, or dads. We have even seen this thinking in our society over the last 100 years. How many Puritans or Puritan churches do we see in America today?

In America's early history, only men with Christian values and public conversation about those values were given opportunity to be in public office to represent our nation. Again, over the course of history, those standards have changed, because of one compromise in 1662 that only a handful of people even knew about.

There is a coin in the British museum in London that was stamped during the reign of Emperor/Pope Constantine that reflects the thinking of that day. It reveals the blend of the church in Constantine's day with the paganism practices. On one side of the coin are Christian emblems and on the other side are emblems of heathen gods.

During the next three centuries, many antichrist ideas entered the church and became the rituals and traditions. The church was robbed of its power, favor, and effectiveness, because of it. We see this still in our churches today. A prime example is the evolving of the Catholic Church and how they have become shrouded with secrecy and mysticism, which Jesus NEVER would have allowed. Everything began to look like Babylon all over again with Pergamum as the new Babylon.

Today, the world has become like Babylon lifting up anything and everything but Jesus.

Some of the ideas and traditions began during Constantine's rule, such as the Chaldean Tau, which is a "T" on the end of a pole, and later was changed to represent a cross. The catholic rosary, which began its history as a pagan method of prayer, was introduced under Constantine's rule. Later, celibacy of priests and nuns was introduced and none of it is biblical; it comes out of paganism. <u>In fact, God said in Genesis, "Go and reproduce your kind"</u>. Celibacy originated with the Vestal Virgins of paganism. Then, in 375, the Roman Catholic Church began to worship the dead, followed by the worship of Mary, hailing her as the mother of God in 431.

Finally, the ultimate paganism ritual was the declaration in 1870 that the Pope was infallible. The word *infallible* means *not capable of making any mistakes or ever being wrong*. It means *perfect, foolproof.*

With the idolization of Mary in the Roman Catholic Church, in 1965, they gave her the title Mother of the Church, and then most recently named her as Queen of Heaven. In case you missed that, she was the human mother of Jesus, **the son of man**, <u>NOT the mother of God</u>. Jesus is the creator of the church.

As evidenced from the many rituals and traditions, it is evident that the church has become more Roman and less Christian, since Constantine's reign in 312 A.D. The Roman soldiers worshipped a god who was attached to the business of war, and today our country has attached its government and its business, to a god of the same thinking—what must we do to get our way, no matter what? As the church declined in all things that are holy and heavenly, it became married to the government or elevated by the government. The Roman Catholic Church became the state religion; the same religion that led to the Protestant Reformation.

The Catholic Church was so full of itself and evil men with evil ideas that men were forced to rebel, if they wanted to follow Christ. It cost those who rebelled a high price in the natural, but they received a grand reward in the spiritual. The Catholic Church literally owned and sold land and people as they became rich and powerful. Many of the priests, who were originally married when the pope passed the law that all priests divorce, did not comply, so the pope had their wives and children sold into slavery and the church kept the money. Can you imagine serving the church and giving it all that you have day in and day out, only to have the leadership and rulers take away the very thing that you loved the most? This is what happened to those priests who did not comply, yet the church succeeded. Its success under Constantine made the people and the presbytery think the kingdom of God had been ushered in, and Israel was out and cast away. This is the point in history where <u>Replacement Theology</u> began, which is absolute nonsense.

Replacement Theology

At this point in history, the replacement theology concepts began. **They thought they were living in the Millennium—really?** It was the church at <u>Pergamum</u> and churches like it that ushered in the 1000 years called the Dark Ages, from the 5th to the 15th century. The years prior, men like John Wycliffe and

John Hus were burned alive at the stake by the Roman Catholic Church, because they dared to make the Bible available to the common man. During this period, people did not have access to the Bible, and by all accounts, it appeared as though God had turned His back on His church. We see this same scenario in the church in America today as indulgences of the members are off the charts as they chase after every desire they have.

Though it did appear that God turned his back on His people, John explained in *Revelation 2:17* that God did not. God provided a means for us to understand that there is hope regardless of the situations we face. There is hope for every circumstance, obstacle, and setback we walk through. John writes, *"To the one who is victorious, I will give some of the hidden manna. I will also give that person a white stone with a new name written on it, known only to the one who receives it"* (NIV). <u>The manna</u> Jesus is referring to is similar to the manna in the wilderness, giving food, and to the bread of life, <u>who is Jesus</u>, but what does he mean by the white stone?

John 1:42 explains that a white stone was given to criminals who had been tried and released as innocent. It was a <u>stone of acquittal</u> and could be shown at any time to someone who accused an innocent person of crimes that were no longer held against them. They were now walking in victory! John began *Revelation 2:17 (NIV)*, "To the one who is victorious." What hope he gave us in that one statement alone. Victorious! We have victory over everything we face. We just have to stand in the victory and walk it out.

<u>Pergamum</u> is a representation of churches both then and now that the Balaam spirit has made inroads and holds influence. It's the idea of "we will do whatever we must to gain the edge over others, and we will compromise and lift up doctrines that justify our position." This is such an accurate reflection of the world right now.

THYATIRA: THE LOST CHURCH

CHAPTER 6

Church of Thyatira

The next church that John writes to is the church of Thyatira, a church that lost its way. Historically, this was the smallest of the other churches, but the letter that Jesus had John write, was the longest. In this letter, Jesus referred to Himself as "The Son of God."

As John begins this letter, he describes the Son of God, "whose eyes are like blazing fire and whose feet are like burnished bronze." His eyes gave the appearance like blazing fire; actually, that translates to "burning coals." His eyes burn away the fog of the mind and the dross that keeps people from seeing truth. Have you ever read something that appeared to be saying one thing, but actually meant another? Then, when you read it again, you gained the full understanding of what was being said? This is what John was referring too. When you see things <u>through the eyes of Jesus</u>, the fog of the mind is removed, and it helps you see the truth.

Then, John's description turned to the feet of Jesus as he described the appearance. They "are like burnished bronze." John does not say they ARE burnished bronze, but he says they looked like burnished bronze. They appeared to John like a furnace of molten metal, they were so bright. Wherever they stepped, nothing would remain the same, as they would crush and then burn whatever and whomever they came in contact with. What John was seeing was a picture of judgment. This judgment was fierce and intense for misleading the people.

The name <u>Thyatira</u> comes from two words that mean *continual sacrifice*. **A continual sacrifice is heresy and pagan.**

Jesus died and became a sacrifice, <u>once for all</u>. The Church of Rome denies, even today, the finished work of Christ and believes in a continual sacrifice and penance. They practice the ceremony of Sacraments that is regarded as an outward and visible sign of inward spiritual divine grace. The act of penance is practiced by man working to convince God that he is worthy of divine love, because he walked up the stone stairway of Peter's Basilica on his hands and knees, and they are now full of blood and pain. Pope John II stated on August 4, 1999, "Today, it would take seven years off his time in Purgatory."

Other forms of penance include, praying for the dead to get early release from purgatory, burning candles, climbing steps on your knees, or beating your back until blood runs down it. We call these the works that man does to add to what Christ has already done. All of these come from paganism as their beginnings were in Babylon. There is NO scripture to back them up. All of it stems from the spirit of the Nicolaitans. Its design is to conquer man and be lord over him. However, we know the truth. There is no other way and Jesus said so. *Ephesians 2:8-9*

(HCSB), "For you are saved by grace through faith, and this is not from yourselves; it is God's gift – not from works, so that no one can boast." And then in *John 14:6 (NIV), "Jesus answered, 'I am the way and the truth and the life. No one comes to the Father except through me'".* No penance, no purgatory, no buying your way out of your sins as the Roman Catholic Church has done for centuries.

As Jesus continues to address the church of <u>Thyatira</u>, He gives them six commendations. The first thing He revealed about the church is the love they had for their fellowman and their deeds. During this time in history, this was a most uncommon attribute, once there was little regard for taking care of people who were sick or different. Jesus spoke about their works, though it does not say what their works were. One can imagine what their works would have been by the way they cared for the needy. They truly were a church with a heart of love, since this was one of the first things Jesus addressed, I believe it was one of the most important things this church did.

The next thing Jesus revealed was the service they exemplified. Their service related to ministry, and that was also easy to see, because Jesus said that He knew their charity or love. Faith was the next thing revealed. Then Jesus addresses their patience or perseverance. Perseverance means a great deal more than patience does, so He uses the word perseverance or endurance. The original says, "hupomone" which *means perseverance and endurance under pressure*, and coming out on the other side of it like a horse whose feet and legs are prancing high in victory. The church at <u>Thyatira</u> had stood the test for a long time, or Jesus never would have used the word "hupomone". Then, He goes back to the first thing He said, this is a working church, not a lazy or indifferent church.

Then, the tables turned, and Jesus explained what He had against the church at <u>Thyatira</u>. *Revelation 2:20 (NIV)* says, *"Nevertheless, I have this against you: You tolerate that woman Jezebel, who calls herself a prophet. By her teaching she misleads my servants into sexual immorality and the eating of food sacrificed to idols."* The word <u>nevertheless</u> or <u>notwithstanding</u> denotes that a major change is coming in this conversation or letter. Then He says, "I have this against you." This accusation is hostile, and its meaning takes us in a different direction. He addressed the woman they have allowed to be in charge, Jezebel. She was a false prophet, and her teachings were causing people to wander from the truth and be led astray. Jezebel was teaching the ways of Balaam. Jesus had been using symbolic language, since His first words to John and this is no different. This behavior was leading people into idolatry, which caused them to form an intimate union with the world. Idolatry is the word for *porneuo*, which is a male prostitute, fornication, or the behavior of a harlot. Here Jesus means they have been taught to be a part of the world, a system He saved them from, but they sold themselves to the world system. When we look around us today, we see several denominations beginning to reverse their stand against evil, and now openly accepting evil as being good or okay, but Jesus is letting the church of Thyatira know that this is unacceptable.

Jesus tells John to tell them, "I gave her a season, a time to change." The word He uses here means time as a period measured by the succession of objects and events and denotes the passing of that time, but she chose NOT to change and turn away from her choices of sin.

So, Jesus broke it down for them, Jesus said, *"Nevertheless or regardless of the good things you have done, I have this condemnation against you. You allow a false prophetess, a teacher of heresy and sin to have a platform in the church that has led many away from the truth"* (Revelation 2:20, Paraphrased).

Jesus said *"I have been dealing with her, because of her continued sin. I have given her much time to repent, but now that is over. There is no more time for her or for those who are with her"* (Revelation 2:21, Paraphrased). Judgment is coming to her house and to those who have sinned with her.

In *John 18:36*, Jesus said His kingdom was not of this world, and yet those who ran His church went out of their way, including the Inquisition, to make their kingdoms of this world, pretending to speak for God, just as this evil woman, this teacher of sin had done. Jesus said she is unwilling to repent, and she has brought this church to a place of judgment; you the church knew better, <u>but you did nothing about it</u>, and even gave her a platform to spread her lies. She is going into tribulation and all those who followed after her will be cast alongside of her. If you are listening to my voice, then please give heed to the warning Jesus gave this church at <u>Thyatira</u>.

Then, Jesus addresses those who are in Thyatira who did not hold to Jezebel's teaching. He basically told them not to become entangled with any ecumenical movement, and soon they would pop up all around them.

Ecumenical means *representing a number of different churches*, **all embracing, and all-inclusive; a universal, non-denominational assembly of different ideas, being embraced by its membership.**

The current pope is working daily to make this happen. One of his predecessors, Pope John 23rd said, "All of us should be one, unbelievers, Protestants, Catholics, Muslims, alike." <u>Religion can do that, but faith and relationship with Christ CANNOT</u>.

Jesus explains in *Revelation 2:23 (NIV)*, "I will strike her children dead." According to Greek Scholar Vincent, this is not a reference to mortal death, but to the Second death, the burning in the Lake of Fire, and I agree, because everyone dies; *it is appointed unto man to die and after that the judgment, so*, this is definitely a reference to the second death in hell. All who appear at the judgment seat are lost, and they are standing there, because they refused to accept Jesus and make Him **Lord,** as well as Savior. Remember, the Balaam spirit is do what you want in order to get what you want; whatever it takes to get your way, so that you can have what you want.

We can see the <u>Balaam spirit</u> in Jezebel as she was teaching the selling of one's soul for whatever the person wanted to fulfill a perceived need. On the other hand, the <u>Nicolaitan spirit</u> is the spirit that wants to conquer others and keep them in subjection, either through ignorance, fear, or misrepresentation.

DR. DAVID DEL VECCHIO with DIANE BRILEY

SARDIS: ALIVE, YET DEAD

CHAPTER 7

Have you ever been in the midst of believing something only to find out you were misled? This is exactly what happened to the church of <u>Sardis</u> when Jesus told John to write to them. Jesus wanted to remind them that there is only one Holy Spirit, and all spiritual life is created by Him. In the midst of John's writing, Jesus tells him to write the most direct and condemning thing he has said to any of the churches, *"I know your deeds; you have a reputation of being alive, but you are dead."* Wow! The church of Sardis operated and acted as though they had it all together, as though they were moving and flowing in the Spirit, YET, Jesus tells them that they are dead. Jesus knew exactly where they were, He saw everything they had done and what they were doing. They were known as a church that was alive, BUT He told them that they were dead. That had to be a tough one, especially when you think you are in the midst of what the Spirit is doing, and you find out from the source that you've missed the boat, but I think we have <u>all been there</u> at some point in our Christian walk.

Sardis

The church of <u>Sardis</u> received the shortest commendation of all seven churches, and it ended up being a reprimand. So, it truly may not have been a commendation at all, as it led to a condemnation, *"You have a reputation of being alive, but you are dead."* Then, the Lord gives them five commands in *Revelation 3:2-3 (NIV)*, *"Wake up! Strengthen what remains and is about to die, for I have found your deeds unfinished in the sight of my God. Remember, therefore, what you have received and heard; hold it fast, and repent. But, if you do not wake up, I will come like a thief, and you will not know at what time I will come to you."* Jesus told the church to wake up, strengthen what is left, recall what you received before, obey it, and repent.

The first command Jesus gave was to wake up. He was telling them that they allowed themselves to fall asleep, no one else did that to them, they did it to themselves. Then he encouraged them to strengthen what was left, plug the holes, or stoke the fire, and bring life back from the ashes. Jesus was close to removing His Spirit from this church. As Jesus continued, He provided a means for them to accomplish this. He told them to recall what they received before, to think back to what they were taught in the past, bring it up to the front of their minds, and then act upon it. He then told them to obey it, and do what they were told to do before, and finally, repent, turn around and go a different direction.

This process is one all Christians need to remember in our daily walk. It is so easy to lose sight of direction in which the Spirit of God is moving as we focus on situations and circumstances around us. We need to always be mindful of what the Spirit is saying to us.

Often, we get into a rut and can't see a way out, or we get stuck doing the same things over and over again, because that's what we've always done. So, we have to keep vigilant, stay aware and keep moving forward with the Spirit of God as we live and breathe in Him.

As Jesus continues with the church of Sardis, He gives a warning; he tells them, *"If you do not wake up, I will come when you least expect me to come" (Revelation 3:3, Paraphrased).* Sardis was a sinking spiritual ship with holes that were letting in water as the ship was going down. It was also like a blazing fire that was allowed to go out, and no one thought to add more wood, or to keep it close to the center so that the fire would stay hot.

The picture of the church of Sardis, based upon their behavior is this; too many people thought someone else would do it. By having that mentality, nothing got done, nothing was accomplished. They thought that,

> "Oh, someone else will pay the tithes and give the offerings, someone else will teach the

children, I can just come and sit and do nothing, but enjoy the fruit of other people's labor and commitment."

"Someone else will invite people to know Jesus, and invite them to church, I have other things that I need to be doing."

This is much like the churches in America today that they have the mentality that someone else will do the work.

This results in churches that are a lot like the church of Sardis, where people say, "Someone else will do it, I have more important things to do." Woe to these churches, they will hear the Lord speak these words back to them. How sad to know that you can feed the fire or plug the holes, but you don't have the heart or interest, or the care to do <u>what only you</u> have been called to do. Their works were empty and fruitless. Their work had not been what God expected or better said, demanded of any of His churches.

Jesus had already spoken about this kind of church, when He walked the earth as a man. Matthew portrayed this for us in his gospel, *"Not everyone who says to me, 'Lord, Lord,' will enter the kingdom of heaven, but only the one who does the will of my Father who is in heaven. Many will say to me on that day, 'Lord, Lord, did we not prophesy in your name and in your name drive out demons and in your name perform many miracles?' Then, I will tell you plainly, 'I never knew you, away from me, you evildoers!"* (Matthew 7:21-23 NIV) Jesus is talking about individual people, as well as people within the church, who are hollow and empty, and without purpose. People or churches who are persecuted, either become tenacious, intense, devoted and persevering for Christ, or they become apostate and walk away from the truth in compromise of what they know is right. When put to the test, their true nature comes out, those who are doing lip service often react by backing away and blending in with the world. Their behavior reveals only a head or brain connection to Jesus, not an ongoing spiritual connection or relationship. To these types of people, Jesus said, "I will deny you before God and the angels."

Here is a church that is practicing and teaching deception. They cause many to fall away because what they teach and believe is foolishness and deception. The worst of all behaviors in a church is rotting from within, dying within and allowing it not to matter.

Jesus reminded us in *Revelation 3:3 (NIV)* to, *"Remember, therefore, what you have received and heard; hold it fast and repent."* We need to remember what was being perfected in the past and decide to repent.

As John continues the letter to the church of Sardis, Jesus reveals that not all who are there have strayed, there are some who have remained faithful. *Revelation 3:4-5 (NIV)* states, *"Yet you have a few people in Sardis who have not soiled their clothes. They will walk with me, dressed in white, for they are worthy. The one who is victorious will, like them, be dressed in white. I will never blot out the name of that person from the book of life, but will acknowledge that name before my Father and His angels."* The Lord has given those who remain faithful a promise, they will walk with Him in heavenly places.

There are many stories about people who have been persecuted, and martyred for remaining faithful, as we are seeing this more and more in our society today. Some may ask, "Why doesn't God stop these sick, perverted minds from having their way with the Christians?" That is not for us to say, because He is the one we serve, and it is His choice what happens to the faithful in the end.

There are many stories about the faithful in Christ. Years ago, a young Armenian refugee came to a relief camp and was asked, "Have you been hurt?" Her response was, "I am bearing the cross, I bear the cross of Christ on my body." The relief workers in the medical tent did not understand her, until she slipped off her dress and they saw the wound on her shoulder.

She had been branded like a cow with a hot iron on her shoulder. The wound was very swollen and badly infected. The girl told the workers what had happened to her. Every day, they would say to her, 'Mohammed or Christ'; and on the last day, they branded her with the cross. She said, "Now every day for as long as I live, I will bear His cross on my body, and someday, when I see Him, I will be glad." This young Armenian girl refused to surrender to her torturers the Savior she served so well.

Today, in our society whether in offices, schools, homes and the workplace, many Christians remain silent and without a voice that stands up for right, truth, justice, and the God they say they serve, the God who saved them from hell. And the only thing they really have to fear is the fear they carry inside, that says to them, "Stay quiet, so that no one will know you're a Christian, so you will not have to defend your faith, or so they will like you and not make fun of you." I call it convenient Christianity or cowardice in the face of the enemy.

Jesus challenged the church at <u>Sardis</u> to be overcomers, His address was more to individuals, and less to the church in general. They had already been seen for who they were collectively. *He who overcomes* meaning those who are born-again and follow hard after Christ and not blend in with the world will walk with Him. We are reminded multiple times in the Word of God to help us stay steadfast in Him. *1 John 5:1-4* and *2 Corinthians 5:19-21* are prime examples of this truth.

As John continues with the letter, Jesus explains, *"The one who is victorious will, like them, be dressed in white. I will never blot out the name of that person from the book of life, but will acknowledge that name before my Father and his angels" (Revelation 3:5 NIV)*. From this verse, it appears that our names are placed into the book of heaven when we are sent into our mother's womb. Up until we reach the age of accountability, our names remain there, and if we die, we are immediately with Jesus. This verse cancels out man's attempt of infant baptism, which has no spiritual or biblical backup. It's just another work of man, even though their motive is good since they are trying to protect the baby and then the child. Yet, it is just an empty act, another method of how the traditions that started with

Catholicism holds its members captive. It is the first compromise with many to follow.

Is there any way to have your name blotted out of the book of life? <u>According to Scripture</u>, there are three ways to have your name blotted out of the book of life. The <u>first</u> way is if we sin against God our name can be blotted out. <u>Secondly</u>, if we fail to accept Jesus as Savior and Lord. He said, *"I am the way, no man can come to the Father except by Me" (John 14:6, Paraphrased).* And the <u>third</u> way is to add to or subtract from the words Jesus gave John to write in His Revelation to John.

If we go back in history to the days of Moses, we can see where God spoke to Moses about the book. We don't know how he knew about the book, but he definitely knew. *Exodus 32:31-33* (HCSB) states, *"So Moses returned to the Lord and said, 'Oh, these people have committed a grave sin; they have made a god of gold for themselves. Now if You would only forgive their sin, but if not, please erase me <u>from the book You have written</u>,' and the Lord* replied to Moses: '*I will erase whoever has sinned against Me from My book.*'"

As Jesus addresses the people in the Sardis church who have been victorious, He said they would walk with Him in white, because they are worthy. Then He continues in *Revelation 3:5* (HCSB) saying, "*In the same way, the victor will be dressed in white clothes, and I will never erase his name from the book of life, but will acknowledge his name before My Father and before His angels.*" Jesus provided a hope to the people of Sardis when He addressed those who were victorious. Not all had missed the mark, and not all had been walking a path of falsehood thinking they were on the right path, so those who the Spirit addressed in this letter were given an opportunity to turn their lives around and follow after Jesus.

The city of Sardis was located 50 miles due east of Smyrna and 30 miles southeast of Thyatira. The richest man in the world, Croesus lived there. Sardis represented the secularized church of the day hosting the seeker friendly church that was open to all who would come. Their pastor did not correct or teach them to be different in Christ, everyone who attended this church looked the same as those in the world.

Paganism survives in this kind of church because no one challenges them. Worldliness is welcomed and at home here, and there are no notable miracles or changed lives. This church became more ordinary as it became more worldly. This is representative of the church in America today.

PHILADELPHIA: AN OPEN DOOR

CHAPTER 8

The next church that John writes to is the church of <u>Philadelphia</u>. The name Philadelphia given to this city and church has nothing to do with the meaning of the word. Philadelphia actually means *brotherly love*, but this city was far from brotherly love during the writing of this letter. Some commentaries say this was such a city, and so it became the name. The city was founded by King Attalus Philadelphus and was therefore named after him.

John begins this letter by disclosing the author of the letter, *"Him who is holy and true, who holds the key of David."* The key of David comes to us from Isaiah. *"I will place on his shoulder the key to the house of David; what he opens no one can shut, and what he shuts no one can open"* (Isaiah 22:22 NIV). This statement is perhaps an amplification of what Jesus said in *Revelation 1:18* (NKJV), "I have the keys to the death and the Hades." Jesus explained in *John 14:6* (NKJV) that, *"No one comes to the Father except through Me."* He has the keys and with the keys comes the power to grant to whom He will, the abilities and gifts to do what must be done.

As Jesus continues with the letter that John is scribing, He states, *"I know your deeds. See, I have placed before you an open door that no one can shut. I know that you have little strength, yet you have kept My word and have not denied my name"* (Revelation 3:8 NIV). Wow! The church at Philadelphia appears to have gotten it right. When Jesus says, *"I know thy works. I know that you have little strength,"* some would venture to say that they apparently did not have many works and that is why He makes the statement, *"very little power."* I tend to think this is not accurate, because for me it goes against who God is to us in this world. The Lord said He opened a door, and if He opened the door, why would He send them out into the world without sufficient power? He would NOT. Most likely, the church was small in number and did not have powerful associations in the community, and no one in the church had any social prominence or elevated standing in the city, however, this church had been faithful to keep God's word and confess His name before others, so they too could find salvation.

Jesus was explaining to the church at <u>Philadelphia</u> that He had provided a way, because He had given them a door with the key that no one can close, and no one can open. This door was provided through Holy Spirit, because outside of Holy Spirit's touch, no one can lead anyone to Christ.

As a believer, we can't just go off and do whatever we want to do without Christ. Paul is a great example with his deep driving desire to go to Asia. His passion for the trip was so intense, yet Paul was told NOT to go. His disappointment was evident as he made the statement that he was going, but Paul knew the importance of listening to God. He could not just up and leave any time he wanted to and still be effective for the Kingdom. He had to wait on God's timing, wait for His signal to go. The Lord did allow it to happen, but He opened a different place for Paul to go first. Later, He opened the door to Asia as Peter revealed in 1 Peter 1:1 (NIV) when he said, *"Peter, an apostle of Jesus Christ, To God's elect, exiles scattered throughout the provinces of Pontus, Galatia, Cappadocia, Asia and Bithynia,"* which are places Paul began mighty works.

So often we try, unsuccessfully, to take the gospel where we want to go and present it, but we fail and have to learn the hard way. Unless the Lord builds the church, they that labor do so in vain that build it. We have to trust Holy Spirit to our hearts, our circumstances, our life situations to get us ready to receive. If we step outside of it, we could do more damage than good. When the door is opened by God, no man can shut it.

This church already had an open door because they were already using what they had and knew to share Christ, so He was opening the door wider and holding it open on their behalf. Jesus was going to make others submit to this church.

As Jesus commends the Philadelphia church, He says, "You did confess me before men." It reads that they did not deny His name. Literally that is *a litotes*, which is a manner of speech, saying a negative to confirm the positive. Jesus told John to write three things about the church of Philadelphia: you have a small amount of power, you are faithful to give adherence to the Word, and you continue to proclaim My name.

The church at Philadelphia was considered weak, yet Jesus told them to, *"Take Note! I will make those from the synagogue of Satan, who claim to be Jews and are not, but are lying, note this, I will make them come and bow down at your feet, and they will know that I have loved you"* (Revelation 3:9 HCSB). If you remember in chapter 2:9, we saw a number of Jews blaspheming the church and Christ. Here, in this city, Jesus reveals the same kind of people and here again He calls them the synagogue of Satan. They again were claiming to be Jews but were lying and deceived in their hearts. *The church at Philadelphia kept His command to endure. Jesus promised to keep those alive from the hour of testing that was going to come over the earth. He told them that He was coming quickly and for them to hold on to what they had, so that no one takes their crown (Revelation 3:10-11, Paraphrased).*

Jesus used the word hour of testing. Here *hour* means *the period of testing*. Think about the tribulation that Jesus said was coming upon the earth. <u>There has never been a universal time of testing over all the earth</u>. Is Jesus announcing here that the faithful church will be taken out or raptured as some teach the Bible says? There is no word found anywhere in the Bible that says raptured. However, *1 Thessalonians 4:16-17 (NIV)* says, *"For the Lord Himself will come down from heaven, with a loud command, with the voice of the archangel and with the trumpet call of God, and the dead in Christ will rise first. After that, we who are still alive and are left will be **caught up together** with them in the clouds to meet the Lord in the air, and so, we will be with the Lord* *forever."* These three words mean to *snatch away, to remove.* <u>Raptured works for me.</u>

LAODICEA: A LUKEWARM PEOPLE

CHAPTER 9

As John continues in his vision, Jesus tells him to address the angel of the church at Laodicea. Laodicea was located about 40 miles southeast of Philadelphia and 100 miles east of Ephesus. The city of Laodicea was a wealthy city in antiquity and was able to rebuild itself after two years of destructive earthquakes bombarding the city in 60 and 61 AD. The people of the city rebuilt it without any help from the emperor. Once again, John establishes the authorship of the letter as he says, *"The Amen, the faithful and true Witness, the Originator of God's creation says"* (Revelation 3:14 NIV). The word "Amen" means *so be it, what you have heard is true, that is how it is, or that is the end result.* "The faithful and true witness" means *the genuine witness who had been on earth and lived His testimony before men.* This true witness was Jesus, and because of the witness of His life, His testimony is absolutely reliable, as well as trustworthy. The word "Originator" is sometimes translated as *beginning or the first cause.*

The Holman translation of the Bible translates Originator in this verse as *arche, which means beginning* and not originator. This is referenced as well in *Colossians 1:15-16 and John 1:2-4.* There would be no creation without Jesus. We would not be here and by extension, nothing else would be here: no earth, heaven, humanity, words – nothing.

How can anyone in his or her right mind, even with limited intelligence, deny a great creator and believe, even for a second in evolution. They can't! It's too ridiculous to mention more than once. Evolution in and of itself is a religion of choice, designed to find freedom from the guilt and payment for sin, and the responsibility of your acts.

John reveals that Jesus knew exactly where the people were in Laodicea when he said, *"I know your works, that you are neither cold nor hot."* The church was <u>not</u> sitting by doing nothing, they were working. They were very busy <u>but that is just it</u>, they were busy, doing busy things. I'm sure they thought they were doing good attempting to be about the Father's business, however, in doing so, they became lukewarm in their relationship with the Father.

Our works reveal who we are and how we think. They will be used to judge us in the end. It's hard for us to grasp the intensity of these words, but Matthew shows us exactly how it will go. *"Then the righteous will answer Him, 'Lord, when did we see You hungry and feed You, or thirsty and give You something to drink?' When did we see You a stranger and take You in, or without clothes and clothe You? When did we see You sick, or in prison, and visit You? And the King will answer them, 'I assure you: Whatever you did for one of the least of <u>these brothers of Mine</u>, you did for Me'"* (Matthew 25:37-40 NIV).

Then, John proceeds to describe the church of Laodicea painting the picture of *a church who is lukewarm, neither hot nor cold, and because of this, Jesus is going to vomit them out of his mouth (Revelation 3:15-16; John 3:16-17)*. Lukewarm water is called tepid water and is nauseating to drink. He provided a consequence to the believers of the church of Laodicea because they were not walking with Him. They had a different focus and could not see their own pathetic condition. This attitude and behavior is much worse than never having been touched by the word of God.

Many speakers today referred to the church at Laodicea as an apostate church, or the people's church, which means it is no longer God's church. The people had changed it into something else. Timothy reveals an apostate church in 2 *Timothy 4:3-4* (AMP), which says, *"the time will come when they [Christians] will not endure sound doctrine; but wanting to have their ears tickled, they will accumulate for themselves teachers in accordance to their own desires; and will turn away their ears from the truth, and will turn aside to myths."* And again in 2 *Timothy 3:5* (NIV), *"having a* *form of godliness but denying its power, <u>have nothing to do with such people</u>.*" Paul said there will be no lack of religion, but people will deny the true power that is able to transform society for the good, producing peace, righteousness, and justice. The power Paul speaks of is the power of the blood of Jesus.

So, what is an apostate church? It is the blending of man's ideas with God's gospel, the fallen state of the original 1st Century church. In the 2nd and 3rd Centuries, the Roman Catholic Church blended pagan practices by combining the religion of soldiers who practiced Mithraism and Constantine with Sol Invictus with the gospel. Today, some major denominations are doing the same thing. They are blending Islam and the homosexual revolution with the gospel of Christ. Once again, man is worshipping the creature and not the creator. Just as it was then, it is now regarding the rebellion of the church against God and His truth. There is only one way, you don't have to like it or even accept it, but that does not change the fact that's how it is in God's eyes. God sees any form of man blending his ideas with His gospel as apostasy, which is a threat to the body of Christ.

The church at <u>Laodicea</u> was a representation of the general church population in America today; however, today it is much worse. Most people believe their relationship with God concerning His purposes is genuine and hot, but sadly, they are not. Most people are actually lukewarm. We are busy working in the ministry, trying our best to get it right, but missing the most important aspect of our relationship with God, which causes us to be lukewarm. We focus on things that really do not matter like trying to tell others how to live, what they can do and can't do, what to wear, what not to wear, what to say and what not to say. We have taken on the role of Holy Spirit, <u>but that is not our job, it's His</u>. Then, there are others who want to enable people, feeling sorry for those who truly do not want to change, but simply want a handout. We try to help them change, but it doesn't work, because they don't want to change. Only Holy Spirit can come and bring change to a person's life. And then, you have those who are not concerned with anyone else at all, they have no sympathy or empathy for those who are lost and in need of salvation.

Today, the masses follow the least qualified and the most self-absorbed, who are seen and heard teaching that the Bible is not the revealed Word of God, rather, it is man's search for God and is therefore filled with myth, legend, and superstition. That is apostasy. Dr. Norman Vincent Peale, the author of "The Power of Positive Thinking" had these same beliefs.

Dr. Peale announced that, "It was not necessary to be born again, you have your way to God; I have mine." What did Jesus say? Jesus said that *"I am the way, the truth, and the life, no one comes to the Father except through Me"* (John 14:6 NIV). And then, Robert Schuller, the man who built the Crystal Cathedral teaches that the essence of Man's problem is low self-esteem. Nowhere in the Bible does it say that, <u>the Bible says it is pride</u>. Schuller also argues that sin is anything that robs us of our "divine dignity." What is that? The Bible says sin is rebellion against God.

The American society has lost its focus, instead of seeing things through God's eyes, His purposes, and plans, we have exploited sin. We have idolized people, concerns, terrorism, crimes, etc. We have allowed our society to turn our attention away from God to focus on things that non-Christians believe are important causing us to be neither cold nor hot in our relationship with God just like the church of Laodicea. A <u>deceived mind</u> is the only one that can believe you can buy your way out of hell and into heaven.

Can you imagine what Jesus would write to the church today? With the church of Laodicea, Jesus condemned them for being neither hot nor cold. The word hot means <u>boiling</u>, changed, converted and on fire or heated up by the gospel. Cold is the complete opposite, it means never changed, not converted, and never affected by the gospel. When Jesus said, "I wish that you were one or the other," it was an indication of His deepest regret that they had come so far, yet they were so far away. What a fearful thing to fall into the hands of an angry God. The churches in America are nowhere near what He is looking for.

We have wasted enough of this precious salvation and this life changing gospel. We need to turn our focus on Him and His Kingdom.

Pertaining to the church at Laodicea, God did not give up, His love revealed by His grace made another call upon them, if not, this letter would never have been written. Jesus said, *"I am about to act, and it is only, because of My love for you, that I have not acted before now" (Revelation 3:16, Paraphrased)*. God is still extending a hand. He is still waiting for them to move back to Him, He never gave up on them.

When we look at the progression of behavior of the seven churches, we see a pattern. The church at Smyrna was more involved in the world than the church in Ephesus whose behavior was worse. The church at Pergamum was more involved with the world than the church at Smyrna and their behavior was still worse. The church at Pergamum was replaced by the church at Thyatira, which was the church that lost its way. The church at Laodicea was running on neutral and they were spiritually idle with all kinds of programs, activities, committees, and community involvement, but no power in the Spirit. No power to heal or change permanently or raise the dead or even to cast out demons. The churches at Ephesus, Smyrna, Pergamum, Thyatira, and Laodicea were full of people who wanted to be <u>active</u> for God, <u>instead of related to God</u>. They wanted to be covered up with involvement and they ended up being uncovered, without relationship, without Jesus, and the entire purpose of their being. Paul warned Timothy that these people had a social gospel with social action in place of a Bible gospel with social changes. They were more interested in administrating and planning social changes than praying for change and asking God to show them how to use His plan (*2 Timothy 3:5*).

<u>Jesus did not say</u> to the church at <u>Laodicea</u> that they belong to Him, as He does the others, even though they claim Him. They said, *"I am rich, I have amassed fortunes and I do not need anything else" (Revelation 3:17, Paraphrased)*. The church judged itself and gave itself the sentence of acquittal. They basically

said they have need of NOT ONE THING. God responded to what these people were saying in their hearts, just as if they were yelling it out loud. In turn, God said, *"You are miserable liars, lying to your own selves, you wretched, pitiful, poor, blind and naked people" (Revelation 3:17, Paraphrased).* What a declaration and condemnation against each of them. The word "naked" here refers to the church as being uncovered in the spirit, or to say it another way, they were without anointing. The church was deceived, they could not see it for themselves, but God knew. Of course, isn't that the meaning of deceived? Everyone knows that your thinking is wrong, except for you, you don't see it.

The churches in general have deceived themselves. Look around the world today and what do you see and hear that is most predominate? Does it reveal Christ? We see fabulous architecture that creates buildings that are worthy of great photography, and churches that have enough money to buy and do anything they want. They are successful in raising money and yet they have enough already. Most churches have unconsecrated membership who only think of the church or the God they say they serve on Sunday and live the rest of the week unto themselves. They are involved in action without relationship, without heart or spirit.

Jesus speaks to John and tells him to record the truth, write to them and tell them, *"You say, I am rich; I have acquired wealth and do not need a thing, but you do not realize that you are wretched, pitiful, poor, blind and naked."* Jesus was basically telling them, *"You are poverty stricken and too blind to see it"* *(Revelation 3:17 NIV)*. Jesus used five strong adjectives to denounce their thinking and behavior revealing his opinion of them. The saddest thing is their complete ignorance of the truth. This is the clearest example of the predominate number of American churches today, they boast of being rich, yet they are in real poverty. Jesus described them as being wretched, miserable, poor, blind, and naked. Then, He explains how to become rich, *"I counsel you to buy from me gold refined in the fire, so you can become rich; and white clothes to wear, so you can cover your shameful nakedness; and salve to put on your eyes, so you can see" (Revelation 3:18 NIV).*

Jesus revealed His way of overcoming their thinking and behavior. Jesus offered them refined gold, which is the symbol of purity. It has been tried and gone through the flames. Gold makes its owner rich. The gold Jesus was referencing was the gold of life that understands anger, grief, pain, and pressure. Those who possess His refined gold become victorious, and to help them see better, He offered them eye salve that relieves bad eyesight. It's amazing that this city developed an eye salve that was sent over the known world and yet they were blind to their own condition of blindness. He also provided them a solution for their nakedness, which was a white robe that has a purpose.

Matthew tells a story about someone who was invited to be with Jesus and thought he could come and participate with Him in any manner that he chose. This should be a wakeup call to everyone.

A King sent invitations to his wealthy and important guest to come to his son's wedding – they were all pre-occupied and could not make it, so he told his servants to, *"Go to the street corners and invite to the banquet anyone you find. The servants went out into the streets and gathered all the people they could find, the bad as well as the good. The wedding hall was filled with guests, but when the king came in to see the guests, he noticed a man there who was not wearing wedding clothes. He asked, 'How did you get in here without wedding clothes, friend?' The man was speechless. Then, the king told the attendants, 'Tie him hand and foot, and throw him outside, into the darkness, where there will be weeping and gnashing of teeth. For many are invited, but few are chosen'"* (Matthew 22:9-12 NIV). Jesus provided us with access to a wedding robe, and yet we think we have a better way. Many times, in this life we fail to accept <u>His way of thinking</u>, because we think we have a better way. God has provided the wedding robe, why on earth would anyone think they can get into heaven any other way?

The church thought they had no need of anything, that they had all that they needed. After all, they were rich. How can the blind and naked buy anything? How can they buy when Jesus said, *"In truth, you are broke/destitute."* But God made a way. *"Come, all you who are thirsty, come to the waters; and you who have no money come, buy and eat! Come, buy wine and milk without money and without cost"* (Isaiah 55:1 NIV). God made a way. They had been saying that they had grown rich and had need of nothing. Only a fool or someone who is terribly deceived would say such a thing, they were deluded and blind to reality.

Jesus was explaining that they could build buildings, amass fortunes, preach and teach, organize and promote themselves, BUT only Holy Spirit can convict and change. Who is being convicted and who is changing, because of their wealth and because of their acquisitions?

Only Holy Spirit can convict, transform, and glorify. When Jesus referenced their nakedness, it was a direct reference to them being uncovered in the spirit or said another way: they were without anointing, without His presence upon their lives. Jesus was telling them that the shame of their nakedness did not appear. Another way of saying this: The disgrace of being without God's anointing did not show who they were to the world, even though they were doing everything in the flesh.

They may have the gift of pastoring, evangelism, or teaching, but since these gifts were given by God, and He does not take them back, even if they are misused, they have remained upon them. God has recorded in His Word that the gifts are without repentance, which means once He gives them, He doesn't take them back.

This concept is very evident in some of the mainstream churches today as some pastors are teaching and speaking the opposite of what God has written in His word. This is true heresy and blasphemy, yet some have the biggest and wealthiest congregations. How can this be happening? Truthfully, it's because most people want their ears tickled and are afraid to hear the truth of the genuineness of God.

The church at Laodicea is alive and well and can be found in America and around the world. We rarely, if ever, hear about any church that constantly reveals Christ. We see great architecture, fabulous buildings, churches with enough money to do what they want, whenever they want. They have large unconsecrated memberships by the millions – to what end? They are involved in actions, but not in heart and spirit. Instead of revealing Christ and His word, they are revealing that they are lost and undone, racing headlong into hell and denying what God has already declared over and over again. Sadly, they are being followed by millions of people who prefer to be misled than upset their own applecart, just like the church at Sardis when Jezebel was teaching them that it was alright to lie, cheat, steal, and mispresent, just as long as you get what you want. It is the Balaam spirit alive and well in the 21st Century.

The church at Laodicea thought they were rich, because of their wealth and material things. They truly thought God was pleased with them and equated this to their spiritual riches which was a delusion.

THE THRONE IN HEAVEN

CHAPTER 10

It's all about to get exciting as the visions intensify for John. Not only is he seeing what is taking place around him, he is listening to the sounds of heaven unfolding before him. What an amazing privilege John had at scribing the vision that Jesus was giving to him. John got to experience first-hand what Jesus wanted to share with others. As John was taking in all that was taking place around him, he began to experience multiple visions. These visions were ones that only the creator of the world and the creator of the visions could reveal. It is not something that John could come up with on his own or see with his own eyes without the revealing from Jesus. Keep in mind that the main figure in Revelation is Jesus. He should always be your focus when you read His revelation. By doing so, it will help keep the focus of why it was written and what it meant and means today.

A Vision Within A Vision

One of these multiple visions, <u>a vision within a vision</u>, takes place in Chapter 4 of Revelation. The second vision began as John saw a door opened to him in heaven. Someone in heaven had opened a door for John to see what was taking place. When a door is revealed, it always means something is behind the door. Since John said, "There was a door opening before me," we know the door meant that John was being given access to the interior of heaven.

John was invited to come into heaven through a verbal invitation from Christ. He was given an open door, not a window to see through, but a door to walk through, which allowed him to enter.

He was about to write what he saw but was interrupted by a sound similar to that of a trumpet. Notice he did not say the sound was a trumpet sound, he said it was similar to a trumpet. John used the idea of a trumpet to convey that the sound penetrated his very being, not just his ears, like a conversation, but an alarm that would involve all of his senses. John used the word *similar* multiple times as he referenced similarities or actions in the visions. This sound was a call, an alarm, or an awakening in his sprit.

As John heard the voice, he was instructed to, *"Come up, and I will show you what must take place after this,"* (Revelation 4:1 NIV). John was suddenly whisked away in the spirit to heaven. Why? Why couldn't John just watch the vision from where he was on earth? The reason is obvious, John had to gain a different vantage point. From earth, we can only see what is right in front of us at our viewing stand, but from the vantage point of heaven, we can see the parade from beginning to end. This should be the first clear message to all of us who would read this book. We should ask God for illumination to see as John saw. When the voice told John to, "Come up," he was giving John permission to see close at hand what was about to happen. The final statement in *Revelation 4:1*, was written in the aorist infinitive, which indicates these things which John was about to see were a necessity and they had to occur.

These visions, spoken and revealed, are being portrayed through John's eyes. Jesus is showing them to John through his sight and engaging in John's hearing to help the visions come to life for John to experience them as well. It's important to understand you must <u>never use earthly ideas or concepts</u> to explain symbols that John refers to as similar to this or that. When you read Revelation without any preconceived ideas, you will come up with some of the same conclusions that are in this book. Looking at Revelation with a finite mind and trying to make earthly ideas work, within a limited scope of heaven, will result in ideas being so far from the intention of the author, you will end up misleading yourself and others. Symbols are given to serve divine purpose and not all of them can be or will ever be explained while we are here. They are given to show the finite mind of man. Heaven holds what is not explainable to us yet, such splendor that our speech cannot even give it a portion of its majesty, because we are unable to grasp it. More often than not, our explanations cheapen the intent of the symbol and for that reason, we do not need to explain away what we cannot. We must be careful <u>not to</u> make more out of the symbols than is stated as has been done by so many. When we exegete, we must say what is and allow that to be enough. Too often, we want to bend what we read, and move it to suite our doctrine, and that is blatantly wrong.

Over the years, I have read this book from a historical perspective, and even took courses in it, that explained the book was presented as if we could interpret and rationalize what John had written. When I decided to teach this, I could see that the only way for me to do so was to make it alive right now. I had to stop pretending that an earthly finite mind can give clarity to many things that are purposed to remain a mystery, so, keep in mind, symbols are symbols, they represent something else.

The Throne

When John was in the spirit, he saw the throne of God, displaying God's role, power, and dominion as God. Picture this, John has just entered through the door with the door behind him, and he sees this incredible throne, the likes of which he has never seen or even dreamed before this moment. There is no cathedral, palace, or building of state, but a throne of such majesty, proportion, and splendor, that he has a hard time describing it. His description falls way short of any real description of what he is actually seeing. Remember, heaven and eternity are without time and space, so what John was seeing was a place where time and space do not exist. John was literally living outside the box on this one.

John explains that around the throne of God were 24 other thrones for the 24 elders who were appointed as agents for the Word of God. Notice that Jesus did not give any history to John at this moment as to any names or tribes, or previous function of the 24 elders. Therefore, it must be symbolic. Remember,

Jesus is giving a vision <u>full of symbolism</u>, such as lamp stands representing churches and stars meaning pastors. Here John is referencing the elders, which is derived from the Greek word *presbyters*. A real *presbyter* guards the word and was assigned by God to be responsible for checking to make sure His word was being carried out correctly in the world.

John continues to describe the magnificent scene before him as he references *"the one who sat there had the appearance of jasper and ruby, and a rainbow that shown like an emerald encircled the throne" (Revelation 4:3 NIV)*. In this instance, jasper is a reference to a precious stone and probably not to the jasper we find on the earth. The jasper John speaks of is also seen with the red of the carnelian. Jasper, even on earth is often redder than any other color, but almost always inclusive of an array of other colors. John's description depicted a translucent stone with iridescent rays of color. The stone was translucent. God, who is sitting on His throne, gave the appearance of gems of these colors. John was not saying that God was a gem, He was describing God's appearance shown like the colors of the stones. And then, around God was a rainbow of color that shined like an emerald that encircled His throne. The hues of green radiating like a rainbow were the only words that John could find to describe the sight before him. It may not be too far a thought to think this jasper color John writes about was more like flashes of color we see in brilliantly cut diamonds, reflecting light and color from light. Green is the color of grace, just as the number 5 is the number of grace. Green represents who God is; God is love, John was trying to help us see who God is.

In the 4th chapter of Revelation, John uses the word throne 12 times. That is more than emphasis, that is a statement for which we must take notice. As he described the 24 elders, He explained that *there were 24 other thrones surrounding the one throne. Upon those 24 thrones were seated 24 elders who were dressed in white and had crowns of gold on their heads (Revelation 4:4, Paraphrased).* The white robes symbolize the purity of the role the elders have in heaven, while the golden crowns are symbolic of the role they have depicting their royalty. The word for crowns here is *stephanos* which represents both honor and victory.

As Jesus continues to reveal what John is experiencing, He engages John's hearing. John described that coming from the throne were flashes of lightning and rumblings of thunder. John was hearing the rumbling all around him. In the original writing, the word for rumblings is the word "voices," which in the Greek is "*phones*," meaning *to reveal what is on one's mind.*

God speaks from the throne and His speech appears to be like thunder and lightning. The thunder and lightning in this instance are fact and not symbolism, yet they are heavenly manifestations of God revealing His power and presence. God speaks from the throne and His speech appears to be like thunder and lightning, illuminating what is on His mind. *Psalm 29:1-11* describes the voice of the Lord beautifully, preparing a way for us to almost touch the sounds from the throne.

He also saw seven fiery torches that were burning before the throne, which are the seven spirits of God (Revelation 4:5 HCSB).

Some translations refer to them as seven lamps instead of torches. These seven have nothing to do with the seven lamp stands John saw earlier in the vision. The previous lamps were symbols of churches. Here John references torches that are lamps of fire. The Spirit Himself is what John is seeing in these seven torches. Holy Spirit, who, when He leaves the throne carries with Him or in Him seven torches or seven spirits of God, because He is God, <u>but only ONE Holy Spirit</u>. So, the seven spirits before the throne of God are the Holy Spirit before He goes out on a mission from the throne. Consider *Acts 2:17 (NIV)* as we read, *"In the last days, God says, I will pour out my Spirit on all people. Your sons and daughters will prophesy, your young men will see visions, your old men will dream dreams."* **What was seen above the heads of the 120 in the upper room? Flames of fire, torches of fire. This was a representation of Holy Spirit on a mission from the throne** *(See also Joel 2:28).*

As John continues to describe what he is seeing, we get a glimpse of the massiveness of his vision, *"In front of the throne there was what looked like a sea of glass, clear as crystal"*

(Revelation 4:6 NIV). Let's take a look at the "sea of glass" that John describes. As John looks at the view before him, he is describing as best he can what he is actually seeing, which is "something like" a sea of glass, that is "similar" to crystal. He doesn't say he is actually looking at glass or crystal, only referencing "the sea" as being transparent, similar to crystal.

Jumping ahead to *Revelation 15:2 (HCSB)*, John describes another sea of glass. *"I also saw something like a sea of glass mixed with fire, and those who had won the victory over the beast, his image, and the number of his name, were standing on the sea of glass with harps from God."* The sea is clear, so you can see through it. How deep is it? And how far does it go?

People who are standing on it appear to be standing in fire, and yet no one seems concerned or affected by it. Could it be what appears as fire are the facets of light reflection like a diamond? A symbol of something we are not yet meant to understand.

As John referenced the sea or glass, similar to crystal, keep in mind that those were the only elements he could use to scribe the scene before him. Remember what we learned about the time and space in heaven. In God's concept, we are all near to the throne and all around the throne, no one is closer to the throne than anyone else, because there is no time and space continuum. There is no distance mentioned. To put all of this into time and space, defeats the purpose of John's vision and rulership of the throne and the power coming out of the throne. Remember, this vision within the vision is about the Throne, keep that in mind.

After John references the sea of glass, He describes, *"In the center, around the throne, were four living creatures, and they were covered with eyes, in front and in back"* (Revelation 4:6 NIV). Notice, John references the four living creatures as being in the middle and around the throne, but remember, there is no space and time continuum in heaven. It is difficult for us to understand the time and space continuum because we live in time and space, but heaven has neither. How can it be that the living creatures were in the *middle and around the throne* with space as it is on earth? How can they be in the throne and around the throne at the same time?

In studying this out, I referenced different commentaries on it and what I found was absurd. One referenced a beast in front of the throne and two on each side and one just above the throne. Really? Where does that come from? The commentaries are seeing this with the natural eye of man and not giving any consideration that in heaven there is no space, as we know it, and no time. Simply put, see it or read it, just as John wrote it, "In the middle of the throne and encircling the throne were four living creatures." These four living creatures were ones that John had never seen before and could only compare them with what he had seen on earth. It could be that they were occupying the same space at the same time since they are not subject to the laws of earth space and time continuum.

Some translations of the Bible refer to the "living creatures" as "beasts". This is a poor choice to translate the word, *pzo'-on*, which means *something that is alive, but not understood*. How any translator could take that meaning from that word and come up with beasts reveals a lack of true understanding of what they were reading. Our earthly descriptions often times take away from the true meaning of what John has written. Some of it remains a mystery.

Most commentators are trying to use their finite minds to describe what John, who saw it, could not describe. They make comments like, "John was first century and we are 20th century, so we have a better understanding; we know more." How can someone who did not see what John saw have a better concept of what he sees than John who is seeing it?

What difference does the century have that makes someone now look smarter than John, because he sees a helicopter or a Howitzer or a space-bot, and now he can explain what John was seeing? He is trying to make it fit into something he did not see. Most of what I have read as an explanation NEVER considers that God has not yet revealed these creatures that He has made, because their time has not yet come. Many of our earthly descriptions do not add, they merely take away, because we are not to know or understand all that John saw. Even Paul was told to keep to himself what he saw, because no one would understand it, and they would try to explain it away. It is too awesome and to out of this world. We do not have to explain it and cheapen a blessing, and the mystery that was meant to remain a mystery until God chooses to reveal it.

Then, in describing the living creatures, John said they have, *"Eyes in front and eyes behind. The first living creature was like a lion, the second was like an ox, the third had a face like a man, the fourth was like a flying eagle"* (Revelation 4:6b-7, Paraphrased). Notice that John's description of the first living creature was like a lion. He does not say the first living creature had the face of a lion. The second like a calf. The third had the face of a man, but no mention of the rest of his body. And the fourth was similar to a flying eagle, with such eyes they are always ready, and always on guard to see and know what must be seen, nothing is hidden from their view.

Once John gives a description of what he is seeing, he explains what he is hearing. *"Each of the four living creatures had six wings and was covered with eyes all around, even under its wings. Day and night they never stop saying: 'Holy, holy, holy is the Lord God Almighty,' who was, and is, and is to come"* (Revelation 4:8 NIV). The fact that they cried, "Holy, holy, holy" could be a reference to the Trinity. Holy is God, Holy is Spirit, and Holy is Son, who was and is and is to come. Once again, Jesus allows John to hear the cries, thus engaging John's senses.

Isaiah and John both saw and described the same living creatures. Isaiah described it this way; *"In the year that King Uzziah died, I saw the Lord, high and exalted, seated on the throne; and the train of his robe filled the temple. Above him were seraphim, each with six wings: with two wings they covered their faces, with two they covered their feet, and with two they were flying. And they were calling to one another: 'Holy, holy, holy is the Lord Almighty; the whole earth is full of his glory'"* (Isaiah 6:1-3 NIV). The word for *train* that Isaiah used referenced all that is around the throne of God, all that borders the throne, filled the temple. From the throne reaching out into the temple area, the skirts of His robe, and all that is contained with them. Then, above the throne, Isaiah saw standing Seraphim; each one had six wings. They were crying Holy, holy, holy. This vision terrified him as he wrote "I am undone." Could Isaiah have seen what John saw? Perhaps. Isaiah called what he saw fiery, burning creatures, the word is Seraphim. John called what he saw living creatures. They both could have seen the same thing.

Some have referred to those around the throne singing 'Holy, holy, holy' as the voice of many angels, but that is not accurate. Jesus had John separate the angels and the four living creatures and elders when he wrote this work, so that the reader would know the <u>creatures and angels are not the same</u>. *"Then I looked and heard the voice of many angels around the throne, <u>and also</u> of the living creatures and of the elders. Their number was countless thousands, plus thousands of thousands"* (Revelation 5:11 HCSB). The four living creatures, once again, are not angels.

As John is observing what's taking place, he notices that *"as the living creatures give glory, honor and thanks to Him who sits on the throne and who lives for ever and ever, the 24 elders fall down and lay their crowns"* (Revelation 4:10, Paraphrased). They are worshiping the Lord in harmony. They fall down before Him and cast their crowns at His feet. What an intimate moment John was observing. I can only imagine the feeling of what he was experiencing as he watched this all unfold before his eyes.

The 24 elders were wearing and casting their crowns before the Throne. The crowns are symbolic of victory and honor, and the word crown comes from *stephanos*, which reveals the royal position of the 24 elders in heaven. I have contemplated the casting of the crowns and have come to some thoughts: Either the crowns that are cast before the throne are divinely replaced upon their heads after each casting, or they are casting or laying at the foot of the throne their honor, victory, and royalty. Otherwise, they somehow miraculously get off their thrones, go over and pick up their crowns, put them on their own heads and throw them again.

As we conclude John's vision as described in Chapter 4 of Revelation, I'd like to make some observations with you. <u>There is no mention of the church</u> in this vision that John has given once we move out of Chapter 3. Could it be that John, as a representative of the church, has been caught-away or raptured as a symbol of the church? Remember, this book is full of symbolism. Is this promise to John a promise to the church of rapture before the great tribulation? Does the matter of the church stop at the end of Chapter 3, some say it does?

1 Thessalonians 4:13-17 talks about those who are asleep being brought to God through Jesus, and those who are still alive would have no advantage over those who have fallen asleep. I have no way of knowing for sure, but I can say that Revelation speaks about the church from chapters 1-3 and after that it does not mention them at all from chapters 4-18. In the first three chapters, as we have already seen, we find seven different churches with seven different behaviors that are symbolic of seven different <u>church ages</u>. Then, from chapters 4-18 we see descriptions of tribulation. There is a great use of Old Testament language in these later chapters that was not used in the first three, as we will see.

THE SCROLL AND THE LAMB

CHAPTER 11

As John's visions unfold, we need to remember that he is seeing visions within visions. In his first vision, he sees God on the throne, and in the second vision, within this vision, is the Lamb that was slain.

Chapter 5 of Revelation begins with John seeing a scroll in the right hand of the One who sat on the throne. This scroll had writing on the inside and outside and was sealed with seven seals on the outside. When I hear or read the words written on the inside and the outside, and then sealed, it means to me that there is no more to say. God said what He wanted to say and no more needs to be added. The scroll that was sealed with seven seals is going to be opened, but we never read anywhere what was written on the scroll. Remember, this is a book of symbols, so we need to focus on what John is focused on. This is another vision within the vision and all focus for John is on what appears in front of him now.

John describes that he sees a mighty angel proclaiming in a loud voice, *"Who is worthy to break the seals and open the scroll?"* As the angel heralded his message, he is the voice calling out to everyone everywhere. His stance and position are very important for us to see that the call goes out to <u>everyone</u>. When he asked who was worthy, He was looking everywhere to see if he could find one who was worthy, *"but no one in heaven or earth or even under the earth is worthy to open the scroll"* as John wrote (Revelation 5:3, Paraphrased). Then, John began to sob uncontrollably and experienced genuine grief. Why did this affect him so? Why was he weeping? John and Jesus' relationship was very close as John knew Jesus as a dear older brother and mentor. John was well aware that the vision he was viewing, and experiencing was from Jesus.

The word for weep used here is *klaio* which means *more than shedding tears* and includes a very external display or expression of grief. He is lamenting with the same kind of emotion someone has when they lose a loved one by death.

The Lamb

John was so distraught because he could not see anyone who could open the scroll. There was no one. The word for "no one" is *oudeis* and it means *no person, thing, or possible way*. This word is used, because the design of the conversation is to reveal the impossibility of anyone or anything upon the earth, or in the heavens or even under the earth opening the seals. If that is the case, then the vision with the seals will never be revealed. John sees the enormity of this and is filled with grief, because John knows how important it is for someone to open the seals. The one who can open the seals is the only one who can pronounce what is in the scroll and cause what is on the scroll to manifest. Whatever is written in the scroll must be spoken. In fact, the words must be planted in the earth, so that they can grow, because all that has taken place before this moment was spoken into existence or planted before what is written in them can happen.

Then, *one of the elders speaks up and tells John to stop weeping and explains that the Lion of the tribe of Judah, the Root of David, has triumphed, he is able to open the scroll and its seven seals (Revelation 5:5-7)*. Remember we talked about the word for elder in Greek is *presbyters*. The *presbyters* are the ones who watch over the word, whether on earth or in heaven. This elder tells John the Lion of the tribe of Judah can do this. In the New International translation, it states, *"See, the Lion of the tribe of Judah, the Root of David, has triumphed" (Revelation 5:5b NIV)*.

I have some difficulty referring to Jesus as the root of David, which is so commonly translated, since Jesus came after David. The word translates as <u>offspring or descend</u>ant, and it is better to translate it as was intended. A possible translation of this word should say *shoot or sprout* because it comes from the root. This is the substitution of the name of what something actually means when speaking, referring to something by the name of its parts, i.e., White House or Administration meaning the same thing. The branch or fruit does not generate the root, the root generates both. However, the root of David, in the spiritual sense was Jesus, and when we read it in the Old Testament, it is always a messianic reference. The word *see* or *behold* is in fact the word for, *let me call attention to something that is external* that you have not yet seen.

So, here is the vision before us, in the midst of the throne, we find the four living creatures, the 24 elders, and God seated on His throne, and then appears another vision in the midst. John is looking, and then he sees it; it appears broken and bruised, hurt as though it had been slain. He sees the Lamb, standing in the center of the throne. Remember there is no time and space in eternity as you see this in your mind's eye. An example of what John is seeing would be a picture that has another picture superimposed upon it or double exposure. In this case, picture several pictures that have been <u>superimposed upon the first picture</u>. All the things that John has seen before are still there, but they are not prominent in this portion of the vision John is having. This vision is about the lamb that was slain, who is in the middle of everything, yet occupying its own space and not forcing any other creature or elder out of their space. There is no difficulty seeing this in your mind's eye when you see this vision in relation to what is around the throne.

Consider this with me: God is upon His throne and Jesus is upon it with Him and Jesus is full of Holy Spirit, so the trinity is upon the throne all at the same time. Jesus, as the Lamb slain, stands up, in His deity, and places in His hands the scroll that contains all the words written by the Father, Son and Spirit that complete the message, and He moves at this time from His position as the Lamb to the conquering lion, who was, who is, and who is to come.

This lamb, this shoot or offspring of David is the one who can open the seals. How does a lion get to be called a lamb? In my opinion, the lion is a conqueror, and the lamb is the one that provides life for others after his death. It seems to be an oxymoron or a paradox that one personality can be both a lion and a lamb. A paradox is a statement that leads to a conclusion that is unacceptable or doesn't make logical sense or it contradicts itself. An oxymoron is a figure of speech that contradicts itself, i.e., holy cow.

The lamb John saw had seven horns and seven eyes. This Lamb is symbolic, and the phrase *having been slain* discusses that something happened to it in the past and the Lamb is carrying it all around with Him in the present. Horns in the Bible always mean power, and eyes always mean vision to see, know, and understand the past, present and even future.

Paul explains the power and vision of God in *1 Corinthians 2:9-11*. He says that God has prepared the things that we cannot see or hear or what we cannot conceive. He continues by saying that no one knows God's thoughts except the Spirit of God, and those are revealed to us by His Spirit.

The seven horns and seven eyes represent the seven Spirits of God, which are the spirit of the Lord, wisdom, understanding, counsel, might, knowledge, and the spirit of fear of the Lord. It is obvious that this lamb is alive again, and now has the seven spirits of God upon him, which is Holy Spirit.

This lamb, the one in John's vision, was slain from the foundation of the earth, and is the person of Jesus, His demeanor, and His gentle and quiet spirit. It is his position as the sacrifice for our sins that Jesus took when He was upon the earth. He allowed himself to be devoured by the enemy of His soul until His time came to be the sacrifice or lamb slain from the foundation of the earth. When His time came, He became the lion, the conqueror. The conqueror is His position as Christ, who conquered sin and death and the enemy of His soul. He is both the lion and the lamb.

In *Acts 7:56 (NIV)*, Stephen saw Jesus standing in his vision, just as he was about to die. Stephen said, *"Look, I see heaven open and the Son of Man standing at the right hand of God."* Stephen's vision places Jesus in a position of action. Think about it, when we are standing, we are about to do something, or we are in a ready position. When we see Jesus in Scripture standing, it means He is establishing, confirming, appointing, and judging. When He is seated, He is speaking, or He is done and at rest.

Another thing to notice is a slain or dead lamb does not stand, he lays on his side dead. Again, this is symbolic; these are all symbols of something greater. The name *lamb slain from the foundation of the earth* is like a title. Let me give you a similar analysis of what this name is. A past president or a past governor is called by those titles even after he is no longer in those positions. He is still known by that title because it was earned or established by him before his time in that role ended.

As John continues watching the vision unfold before him, he sees the lamb take the scroll from the One seated on the throne. The idea of Jesus, who is the lamb in the vision, taking the scroll out of the hand of God is a bit disingenuous in its wording. He did take it out of the hand of God as if it was His place to do that. It means to accept or receive as in receiving honor to oneself, coming by your own hand. You may be asking the question,

"How can a lamb take a scroll?" Just remember who the lamb represents; the lamb is a symbol of Christ.

Also remember, what John is seeing is not limited by date and time. We don't know when the Lamb takes the scroll, which means this vision is not dated at the time John sees it. John's vision was given in 95 and has nothing to connect it to a specific date.

After the lamb took the scroll, John saw the four living creatures and the 24 elders fall down before the Lamb. They each had a harp and a bowl full of incense, which are the prayers of God's people (Revelation 5:8, Paraphrased). Picture with me the 24 elders. They all fall down along with the four living creatures, even though John does not speak about them; they are there in the midst. The 24 cast down their crowns before the throne and at the same time each one of them has a zither or harp in one hand and a golden bowl filled with the prayers of the saints in the other. Wow, what a sight. Now, trying to think through this from a logical concept, how can they do this all at the same time? They bow and throw their crowns, and at the same time carry with them a golden bowl with the prayers of the saints and also carry a harp. <u>Very impressive</u>. Here, symbols represent more than physical things. Remember crowns are symbolic of victory and honor which reveals the royal position of the 24 elders.

As John describes the golden bowls of incense in each of the elder's hands, he made a point to include what was in each bowl. His description shows how precious each one truly is. Each bowl was filled with the prayers of the saints that he describes as incense. Incense is a sweet burning fragrance, a lot like perfume. That is how God views our prayers, precious, valuable, and honored as He places them in a golden bowl. The bowls of gold are mentioned only because the prayers must be held in something precious. Prayer in the vision is simply prayer. There are no symbols of something else when John speaks of prayer. Prayer is prayer that enters heaven as the sweet smell of incense.

As the Lamb takes the scroll, John explains the position the Lamb has to open its seals. He breaks it down, so there's no doubt who the Lamb is representing when he says, *"You are worthy to take the scroll and to open its seals, because you were slain, and with your blood you purchased for God persons from every tribe and language and people and nation"* (Revelation 5:9 NIV). The Lamb is worthy to open the scroll and break the seals, because he purchased the right to do this by shedding His blood as a faultless lamb. His shed blood purchased some of every tribe and tongue and nation. It was not His death that purchased them, <u>but His precious blood that paid the price</u>, and became the ransom. He bought us for God with the price of His blood. His role as lamb was determined before the earth was ever formed. Everyone was included in the price, but not everyone wants Him (Matthew 22:14).

THE SEALS

CHAPTER 12

As the Lamb began to open the first of the seven seals, John heard one of the four living creatures say in a thunderous voice, "Come and see!" John looked and there in front of him stood a white horse. The rider held a bow, and he was <u>given</u> a crown. He rode out as a conqueror headed on a conquest (Revelation 6:1-2, Paraphrased). Some say this is a picture of the beginning of Christ's conquering and chapter 19 of Revelation fulfills His task. <u>However, I do not agree</u>. Christ does not move at the command of the four living creatures. He is the Lamb, the only one worthy to open the seals. Why then would he take orders from others who are not as worthy, and who have not paid the price that He did to open the seals? He is God, and He gives the commands.

The first living creature with the thunderous voice was like that of a lion. He is the one who told John to "Come and see." I do not think it is a coincidence that the lion is the one who announced this horse and rider. Really, what John was witnessing was the beginning of a new season, as each of the seals were broken, a new season began, so John saw more than just the horse and rider.

We read about these various seasons throughout the Scriptures. Amos talks about destruction and judgment coming on the day of the Lord for Israel *(Amos 5:18)*. This day will be a day of repentance for many, but not everyone will turn to the Lord. Many will perish.

Another season mentioned this time in the New Testament is the Day of the Lord. This is referred to as the second coming of Christ *(1 Corinthians 1:8-9; Philippians 1:6; 2 Thessalonians 2:1-3)*. The phrase the Day of the Lord refers to periods of judgment. The Scriptures say that the Day of the Lord will come as a thief in the night. When a thief strikes, no one knows he's coming as it is very unexpected. The Day of the Lord is an extended period of time when God begins to deal with Israel <u>after the rapture of the church.</u> During this "day" or period of time, the elements will melt, and the earth and works on the earth will burn up (2 Peter 3:9-10.

As the seals continued to be opened, John saw the Lamb, Christ, the Lion of Judah open the second seal. When He did, the second living creature said, *"Come and see." And a red horse went out on assignment. Then, the third living creature announced the release of the black horse with the one carrying the scales or balances in his hand said, "Come." The fourth living creature announced the fourth horse and rider. This horse was pale and the rider as the spirit of death and the spirit of Hades followed with him (Revelation 6:3-6, Paraphrased).* When the Lamb opened the seals, it was a culmination of history coming to an end.

Remember when the first living creature spoke, it was the sound similar to or like thunder? This was only said once because it was not necessary to say it again. No one could turn away from the scene and no other call was necessary. All four of the living creatures said to the four horses and riders to, "Be going." The four horsemen have been sent out on their assignments to the earth to administer the plan and purposes of God. Notice the assignments of each one.

I'm sure you have heard teachers and preachers talk about Christ being the rider on the white horse. However, since the Lamb, Christ, is opening the seals and the riders and their horses are receiving orders from the four living creatures, it doesn't make sense to say this white horse and rider is Christ, and to place Christ as one of the four others on assignment does not make sense.

The colors that John used to describe the horses are significant, otherwise John would have just said horses. The white horse went out with a rider who carried a bow and was wearing a crown. Notice that this rider was <u>"given" a crown</u>; it was not earned. He was granted permission to use it. He was a conqueror who went out to conquer. Those who become conquered lose their peace and most of the time blood is shed. The red horse and rider have the power to take peace from the earth, and those who are conquered are often killed before those who remain are conquered. These two, the white and the red, were perhaps dispatched together. If God wanted to conquer His children, He would have started at the beginning of the gospel, and instead of salvation being a gift, we would have been conquered, not saved by His grace or love.

In John's description of the rider and the white horse, he used the word "conquering" with the aorist, and "to conquer" in the Greek is a past tense followed by a future tense, which means to *conquer totally and with finality,* yet the rider on the black horse that John describes held the scale of balance in his hand, which means he was about to influence the balance of things. Each of these riders and horses had a specific job they were to fulfill.

Notice that only the last or the fourth horse and rider were given a name; <u>the death</u>. The others did not have a name, <u>only a purpose</u>. A name was given, because they were spirits, and <u>the</u>

<u>hell</u> followed with him. Looking at the original Greek writing, both titles are preceded by a definite article, which indicates a person or entity. Both will be thrown into hell, as they are entities, not ideas or locations.

I believe the white horse and rider represents an imposter, a deceiver. In view of the fact that Chapters 4-20 of Revelation speak of things to come, I hesitate to say with finality that I am correct, because John was told to write what he saw, and John used symbols. John was in the spirit and saw, based upon the Word, what one can only see in the spirit and not as a natural man. Could this white horse and rider with the bow and crown symbolize an imposter, an antichrist appearing as Christ? <u>I think so</u>. Remember, he goes out <u>with</u> a red horse and together they conquer and kill; this is <u>not how</u> Jesus works. He is a redeemer, and the end has not yet come when Christ will indeed kill, not with natural means, but words from His mouth that will be uttered for two hours, when all the enemies of Christ in the Valley of Armageddon will be killed. Jesus came to save the earth, not to destroy it before the time. The devil and his minions, the adversaries of Christ, came to steal, kill, and destroy the earth and all that are in it. The white horse and red horse and their riders are war and death in my opinion *(Matthew 24:4-6)*.

John described the rider on the red horse was given a great sword. We often think of a long and powerful Thracian sword. However, that is not the case. That thinking is earthly thinking and does not see the symbol the sword represents, which is great destruction and death. Looking back at history, we can most likely see its true meaning. **Many leaders in ancient times were known as "So and so the great." Herod the great, Alexander the great, Cyrus the great of Persia, Antiochus the great and Frederick the great, among others. These names were given because they were conquerors or did extremely great things in their kingdoms. For this reason, I believe the great sword means <u>a great death</u> and <u>massive destruction</u>.**

We all hear foolish men without understanding come up with treaties in an attempt to bring peace, but that can never happen as long as men and nations love sin, allow and express hatred, and living in unrighteous behavior. Peace will never happen outside of Christ.

As John is listening to what is going on around him, he hears as though there was one voice coming from the four living creatures say, "*A quart of wheat for a denarius (a day's wage for one man (to eat) with very little left for anyone else) and three quarts of barley for a denarius, but do not harm the olive oil and the wine*" (*Revelation 6:6 HCSB*). It appears that the four spoke with one voice or a voice of agreement about what was to happen next. They spoke it, sent it to the earth; they planted it. Most commentators say this represents famine and that makes sense. However, it lists the cost of food products, but never does it say to hurt the crops. It does say not to harm the oil and the wine. <u>This is not famine</u>; this is something else entirely. As you continue to look at what John is seeing, he describes another horse and rider who does bring famine. So, it's not the black horse and rider. Perhaps, and most likely, it's the destabilization of the economy.

God always fires a shot across the bow to warn before He brings judgment. The unstable economy allows products to still be available, but the prices paid for them are extravagant, so not many people are able to purchase them. The poor would hardly be able to survive, but the wealthy will just spend what it takes to buy what they need. Because of this, I do not believe this is a famine, but extraordinary prices required for the necessities people will need for survival.

Could this be a change in the monetary system that is coming? Possibly. What would happen if there was a sudden change in our economy and things were not readily available as we have always expected them to be? I find it interesting that in 2021, we are experiencing terrible inflation and necessary items are scarce.

In 1929, and several times later, there was a transfer of wealth that changed the economy of America. The market lost 89% of its value. Then, in 2008, the crash of the market was worse than the one in 1929 with people killing themselves, because the stock market crashed. In both eras, people did not think with a rational mind. A rational minded person would have said the companies who represent those stocks are still here, so one day the stock will regain its value. The people who were smart and understood this apparently had saved money and bought stock at bargain prices, and when the prices went up, they became wealthy. In today's marketplace, however, not all businesses will make a comeback, in fact, most will not. The prophets of the marketplace and prophets of the spirit are both saying the same thing: that the greatest exchange of wealth is coming soon. How soon is the question. There is a Jewish phrase that is true: <u>"It is better you should be a year too early than 10 minutes too late."</u> There is another great crash coming and this time the church needs to be the one that receives the greatest transfer of wealth that has ever occurred. Before we spend like we have been doing, we must start thinking what we will do when this happens. This will set us up to be the ones who gain and not lose. When this happens, a lot of the government funded assistance will dry up and no longer be available. The governmental policies and procedures will have to adjust and be amended as the times change. The real problem we are seeing in today's society is the moral collapse of the people who are perpetuating the problem. There have been many calamities historically that created the deaths of millions. We see this vividly throughout the Old Testament with pestilence and plagues, wars, and famines. But all of these occurred in the earth long before the opening of the seals, and the sending of the three other horses into the earth, so, this discussion is not about what has already happened, but about what is yet to come.

Then, as the fourth seal was opened, John heard the voice of the fourth living creature say, *"Come!" And he looked and there was a pale green horse on which the horseman named Death was upon it, and following behind him was Hades. Was Hades riding a horse – how did he keep up? Authority was given to them over the fourth of the earth to kill by sword, famine, plague, and by wild animals of the earth (Revelation 6:7-8, Paraphrased).* This pair brings death and calamity, starvation, horror, and even establishes the inclusion of participation of wild animals like none has ever known to mankind before. These will take place upon the ungodly.

The fourth horse was sent only by the fourth living creature, with all the others in agreement. The seal was opened by Christ as the Lamb, and it was His command to plant this seed in the earth. Keep in mind that Death was followed by Hell (Hades). Death takes the souls from the bodies and Hell gathers those who chose not to accept Jesus, those who thought they had a better way: fools, pretenders, anarchists, and the religious without a relationship with Christ. I believe Christians will die during this period, because Holy Spirit is still at work in the earth, but Hell will not get all of them.

Notice that each of the four horsemen bring judgment to the earth by bringing condemnation and destruction. However, the condemnation is not against the believer who believes in Jesus Christ. John's gospel tells us, *"Whoever believes in Him is not condemned, but whoever does not believe stands condemned already, because they have not believed in the name of God's one and only Son" (John 3:18 NIV).* And again, *"Very truly I tell you, whoever hears my word and believes him who sent me has eternal life and will not be judged, but has crossed over from death to life" (John 5:24 NIV).* John also wrote in Revelation 3:10 *(HCSB), "Because you have kept My command to endure, I will also keep you from the hour of testing that is going to come over the whole world to test those who live on the earth."*

In the Old Testament, Malachi wrote, *"They will be Mine, says the Lord of Hosts, a special possession on the day I am preparing. I will have compassion on them as a man has compassion on his son who serves him" (Malachi 3:17 HCSB).*

We know that since time began, Godly people have died in every manner conceivable, but these deaths are not, because of God's judgment and condemnation. God does chasten and rebuke, and He removes His hand of protection, but for those who have accepted Him as Savior and Lord, He does not condemn *(Hebrews 12:5-6).* There will be a time that the believer in Christ will be judged for his or her own works, <u>but this is a judgment for reward</u>, not condemnation.

By the coming of the fifth seal, souls are revealed under the altar. People were killed for their faith and testimony from all the ages, including those killed after the seals were opened who accept Jesus as Lord prior to their deaths (Revelations 6:9-10, Paraphrased). Are the dead who have been martyred waiting under the altar, while all other saints are free to go throughout heaven?

I believe this must be another symbol that John is using, because I don't see the martyrs staying and remaining under an altar for eons and eons of time, while they wait for the rest of the martyrs to be killed, especially while every other saint moves freely about heaven.

Remember, each of these visions is a vision within a vision, and I believe this one is a separate view of what's taking place somewhere in heaven. No one is killing or martyring believers in heaven, and no one functions as a priest or does the chores of the priest. This altar is not to be compared, as many have done, with the altar of the temple where the priests sacrificed spotless lambs, and afterward washed their blood-filled hands in a laver. So then, what kind of an altar could accommodate such a large number of martyrs? Why do they have to stay under the altar and cry out for release? Are they all huddled under the altar? Are they standing or lying down? Do all the martyrs have to go to this certain altar and wait when they enter heaven? The answer to each of these questions is No. This must be a symbol of their connection to the altar of sacrifice and Christ the Lamb, who was the great sacrifice.

The altar where the blood was shed, and the Lamb have a special connection. To have them hanging out under the altar seems irrational.

John explains that *the martyr's cried out to the Lord questioning, how long it would be until the judgment of the inhabitants of the earth. Then, he saw each of them receive a white robe, and they were told to wait until their brothers and sisters were killed just as they had been (Revelation 6:10-11 HSCB).* Here, John allows the reader to see that the martyrs are not huddled around or under a big altar waiting for the last martyr to be killed. They are connected to the altar and to Christ through His shed blood. <u>It's a reference to a position or relationship to Christ, not a location.</u> This relationship was bought by shedding their own blood and refusing to deny Christ. They died for Jesus, who is the Word of God. To kill someone for confessing Christ is too hideous a crime for me to understand. The killers of these martyrs are screaming out a challenge in God's face, "I do not believe your God exists." That behavior now has the consequences that it deserves, and payback. The martyrs knew that when grace comes to an end, their deaths will be avenged, their killers judged, and sentenced to eternal torment in hell. Time would run its course, and those who killed the servants of God, for standing firm in their faith will stand in their judgment, if not, it would have been written here. The martyrs all died because of the gospel, and their love and faithfulness to Christ. They refused to live as those who denied their master and savior.

If we look at the responses between the Old Testament saints and the New Testaments saints, we see completely different reactions. The Old Testament saints cried out for the death of those who killed them, <u>but not</u> the New Testament saints. Why would they not? Why would they want the lives of those who caused so much harm to their brothers and sisters in Christ not to receive the punishment they deserve? <u>All I can say is Jesus</u>. When Jesus came to the earth, He brought grace. This was His love. He extended so much grace to those who did not deserve it. Grace brings with it time, and an opportunity to accept His grace. Stephen displayed this beautifully in the Book of Acts. As they were stoning him, Stephen cried out, *"Lord, do not hold this sin against them"* (Acts 7:59-60 NIV). Wow, what grace.

The four horses and horsemen were NOT sent against the church. Notice that none of them were killed by the four horses or their riders. The two visions are completely separate. The martyrs are in one and the horses are in another. If they had been included in the deaths brought about by the four horses, they would have known how long it would have been for God to avenge their blood and would not have had to ask, *"How Long?"* *(Revelation 6:10 NIV)*. They would have known how long. That is why I believe they were not killed by the four horsemen. God's response to them was, "Wait a little longer, until more martyrs are killed." God never seems to be in a hurry, He uses time as His tool. Time or the absence of time and eternity are His creations. It took Him 40 years after the Jews killed Jesus, with the help of Rome, before He sent judgment upon both.

The Jews cried out to God because they wanted retribution. They wanted judgment and wanted it so badly that their cry was, "His blood be upon us and our children." God gave them, once again, what they wanted. They received the just reward of their own words, and that reward continues even today all around the world, but they do not connect the dots.

The question we all ask is, "When will the end come?" Matthew and Peter explain this for us *(Matthew 24:23-27; 2 Peter 3:9-10)*. Jesus laid it all out for us in His Word. We just have to look for it. He explained that when all the Gentiles who are going to accept Christ come into the faith, the gospel is preached to all nations, and the imposter, the faker, the usurper, the antichrist has run his course, then the end will come. Supreme governmental control, both executive and judicial, will be wiped out. The people tire of a false government who takes from the poor and middle class, pretending to help them, and gives what it takes from these sheep to give to the privileged. We see this very clearly in our society today.

When John saw the sixth seal open, *the earth began to shake with a great earthquake, the sun turned black like sackcloth made of goat hair, the whole moon turned blood red, and the stars in the sky fell to the earth, as figs drop from a fig tree when shaken by a strong wind. Then, the heavens receded like a scroll being rolled up, and every mountain and island was removed from its place (Revelation 6:12-14 NIV)*. This great earthquake is way more than any earthquake we have ever known. This word means a great shaking so intense that it causes other things to occur.

We can see in the earth today that God is doing a mighty shaking. We see it everywhere we turn.

We often talk about what would happen if an asteroid hit the earth. It's almost inconceivable for us to imagine such a thing. It would move the earth off its axis and change everything: the ocean and tides, the weather and seasons, and day and night. Is that what these verses mean? Or do these stars represent people in high positions as the stars did in the beginning of Revelation? Again, Peter describes this perfectly as he talks about the elements of earth being destroyed. Yet, he also gives hope to those who live a holy and Godly life and the coming of a new day. *"But the day of the Lord will come like a thief. The heavens will disappear with a roar; the elements will be destroyed by fire, and the earth and everything done in it will be laid bare. Since everything will be destroyed in this way, what kind of people ought you to be? You ought to live holy and godly lives as you look forward to the day of God and speed its coming. That day will bring about the destruction of the heavens by fire, and the elements will melt in the heat. But in keeping with his promise we are looking forward to a new heaven and a new earth, where righteousness dwells"* (2 Peter 3:10-13 NIV).

John's account of what he is seeing is very hard to comprehend. In our minds, it is almost impossible for us to see the heavens roll up like a roll of paper. If this is taking place, then where is John? I thought he was in heaven. Where is everything He has already seen going to be? This is obviously beyond our ability to comprehend. Mountains could be large and powerful nationalities and countries. Islands could be small ones that move away from what they once were. Then again, they could be mountains and islands that move a little from where they were put originally and have always been. The possibilities are numerous, but, as we continue to observe the seals, we notice that once the seals are opened, they remain open. They are not closed. This tells us that a certain amount of time is required. Time is the key because there is still time for judgment.

The first five seals reveal a pattern that takes the earth and all that is in it to the end. But the sixth seal talks about the end. When it is opened, time ends, and all that we have ever known comes to an end, heaven does not roll up like a scroll if the universe is to remain intact. John describes that *everyone else, both slave and free, hid in caves and among the rocks of the mountains, whether they were kings, princes, generals, rich, or mighty*, it mattered not their position, *yet these people were not believers. These people called to the mountains and the rocks to fall on them and hide them from the One who sits on the throne, and from the wrath of the Lamb (Revelation 6:15-16, Paraphrased).* Jesus warned Israel about this very thing as Luke scribed in the Scriptures in *Luke 23:28-30*. Why would a believer fear the wrath of God? This kind of fear and terror described here in these verses is coming, and all the evil practices and behavior that have been done in the earth will be judged. Those who are here, because they refused Christ, will feel such a terror that their bodies will quake as if they are literally coming apart.

The judgment that is coming when these seals are open, especially the sixth seal, will be far worse than the flood, or Sodom and Gomorrah. What is coming cannot be survived by anyone, not even the mountains. There will be no coming back for this earth, or those who remain, as they chose to reject God and Christ. This judgment brings together the wrath of God and the Lamb, which carries the full weight of God, the Lamb, and the seven Spirits of God, which is Holy Spirit. They will release their wrath and judgment, and what they created with their own words; this earth and the universe will come to an end as we know it. Today, we are seeing an open rejection by many rulers on this earth, and this rejection is merely a prelude to those who are even more evil, if you can even imagine that.

DR. DAVID DEL VECCHIO with DIANE BRILEY

THE 144,000 SEALED

CHAPTER 13

In the 1870s, a false religion or a cult called Russelism was developed in Pennsylvania. This cult evolved and is now known as Jehovah's Witnesses. The controversary that initially started this religion was over the great tribulation and the 144,000 selected ones who would be going into the millennium. There have been many controversies over the great tribulation and the 144,000 mentioned in Scripture. Jehovah's Witnesses see the 144,000 literally and that's why they work so hard. They believe they can earn their spot if they work hard enough. This is the complete opposite of what the Bible says about heaven, the new earth, and the millennium. Because of these controvarsaries, it is important that we understand these two very key issues, the great tribulation, and the 144,000 for the truth they were intended to be.

Jehovah's Witnesses <u>are not Christians</u>. They believe that Jesus is Michael, the archangel. Their *Watchtower* publication declares that the final number saved in the church will be 144,000, and the rest of those who are saved from hell will live on a glorified earth.

Some other groups argue that this number represents those who will be saved out of the physical nation of Israel. Others feel this is spiritual Israel, the church, and still others think this number of 144, 000 represents a group of martyrs that have given their lives for the cause of Christ. **Just for information, as we look at this, let me share that the term <u>thousand</u> is used 19 times in Revelation, <u>but not even one time is it used as a literal thousand</u>: only a symbolic number.**

The vision John continues to see is expanding, vision upon vision. He sees four angels standing at the four corners of the earth: north, south, east, and west. They are holding back the four winds of the earth to prevent any wind from blowing on land or on the sea. Then, he sees another angel come from the east, carrying the seal of the living God. This angel called out in a loud voice to the four angels who had been given power to harm the land and the sea to STOP! *Do not harm anything until we put a seal on the foreheads of the servants of our God (Revelation 7:3 NIV).* Wow! How powerful. Can you picture it? Everything was stopped, halted, to make sure that God's people were protected and saved from the harm that was coming.

Then, comes the most controversial verses in the Bible. The 144,000 that were sealed. Some believe the 144,000 are Jews only, which is the more common belief. What follows next is very important and very interesting, because over the years groups have sprung up that created religions based upon this scripture. Some have said this seal had been placed upon the 144,000 to protect them during the great tribulation to keep them safe from Satan and the antichrist. <u>If that is so, then who kills them and makes them martyrs?</u> There are seven places within the New Testament that says God is no respecter of persons, so, for these verses, and this 144,000, God is going to break His own word? No way! Some have also written that the servants are sealed, so that God will know who they are during the great tribulation. <u>Really!</u> That means the omniscient God needs a mark to recognize His own children. We know better than that. The Bible reminds us that *<u>the Lord knows those who are His</u>* (2 Timothy 2:19a, John 10:14).

It's important to understand that this is a vision within a vision that appears between the opening of seal six and seal seven. The end of the earth is not allowed to come until all of God's servants are sealed. This part of the vision was not given a chronological order that we can follow, so we do not know when this takes place, only that it takes place. It appears like an anacoluthon; the events are out of sequence. There is no more said about these angels after the opening of the sixth seal or before the end. Like many visions, it is here to complete the vision.

When John references the 144,000, he was basically recording that there is a great multitude of people around the throne. He is trying to give a full description of what he is seeing and hearing. At this point, John does not see the 144,000. <u>He said he, "heard the number"</u> *(Revelation 7:4 NIV)*. It's not until later John reveals that *he saw them with the Lamb on Mt. Zion in Jerusalem, and then in an instant they are in heaven with Him (Revelation 14:1)*.

So, at this point, John is seeing the four living creatures, God, and the Lamb with seven horns and eyes, and the 24 elders all in the midst of and around the throne. Remember, there is no time and no three-dimensional space in heaven. All these heavenly beings are exactly where the Bible says they are, and not one is interfering with the other.

Numbers in Scripture

Numbers are very significant throughout the Bible. Learning to recognize them and what they mean and stand for, helps with the understanding of what is being said. An example is the number 10 expresses <u>completeness</u>, the total sum number - 10x10x10=1000. This number is completeness on the highest level. Remember, John described the 24 elders around the throne, which would be 2x12. Then, with the number 144,000, we have 12x12x1000. It all connects, we just must learn to see the connections. The number 144,000 that John is referencing is symbolic. Looking at some Bible history will help us understand <u>the number is not literal</u>.

There were 10 Jewish tribes of the northern part of Israel who were taken by force to Assyria and made captives. They eventually were absorbed into the culture and became intermarried with pagans. Then, in 70 AD Simeon was absorbed into Judah and Benjamin lost their national existence and never got it back. Yet, the Bible says 12,000 out of every tribe of the sons of Israel. Notice, it does not say that there were some out of one tribe and less out of another. What if 2 or 3 or more from one tribe wanted to be a part of Christ, and 2 or 3 or more from another tribe did not want to be a part of Christ? What then? Yet, the Bible says 12,000 out of each tribe, a perfect number. <u>Again, this is symbolic and not literal</u>. This shows organization of heavenly order, not a haphazard method of the collection of saved souls. Recall how John described *the many angels, numbering thousands upon thousands, and ten thousand times ten thousand (Revelation 5:11 NIV)*. This number of 10,000 x 10,000, ad infinitum, is the complete number of the angelic host. This is not an indiscriminate number, because <u>God does not do anything random</u>. When the 12 tribes were on the earth, their numbers were very different and their reward in the land of promise was also very different. In life, their numbers were never the same and never even.

Looking at the tribes that John lists in Revelation, there are some that are missing *(Revelation 7:5-7)*. Dan is missing, and that is a problem if we follow those who say this represents the sons of Israel. This is not true if one is missing. Levi, who is listed, no longer has a special place on this list among the tribes with God. This could also be a problem if we read it without this consideration. Ephraim is replaced by Joseph on the list, and yet Joseph's other son Manasseh is on the list. Yet, God through Jacob chose Ephraim over Manasseh, and Judah was named before his older brother Reuben. So, as we look at the 12 sons, this list is not correct. Twelve is the number that God uses for His people: 12 sons, 12 tribes, 12 pillars in the temple, 12 apostles, 12 x 2 elders around the throne.

Another thing to consider is why would God give honor to these 12 tribes? When Jacob was blessing his sons just before he died, he told his firstborn son Reuben, "You are unstable as water. You even went up to my bed and took my woman. You defiled me." To Simeon and Levi, he said, "You two are cruel murderers." To Benjamin he said, "You are a ravening wolf, violent, deadly and cruel." I do not see the tribes as literal at all here. They are symbolic.

Seal of God

In earlier verses, we read that the four angels had the power to hurt the earth and the sea. God sent the fifth angel to stop the other four at just the right moment. This could mean that what was coming could interfere with the work of sealing the servants of God. The order by the fifth angel was for the other four to not hurt land, sea or even a tree. No wind was to blow, even to the point of no breeze among the trees. <u>How can the wind keep someone from being sealed?</u> This again is symbolic. No one can see the wind; what we see are the effects of the wind, the aftermath. *"The wind blows wherever it pleases. You hear its sound, but you cannot tell where it comes from or where it is going. So, it is with everyone born of the Spirit"* (John 3:8 NIV).

Take a look at the fifth angel. As John describes this angel, he says the angel is carrying the seal of God in his hand. **<u>The word seal used here is a noun and not a verb</u>, which means he is NOT stamping, branding, or tagging the foreheads of the servants of God.** When the verbs are used here, they say only *to seal* and *having been sealed*. There is no indication, based upon the words used that there is a brand, or a scar placed upon the foreheads of God's servants, but there is something that sets God's servants apart. Here on earth, we do not have any such instrument, so we cannot even compare this instrument that seals with anything on earth, because if we could, we would cheapen its value, and make it comparable with something earthly, and no longer able to hold its heavenly importance.

We have to rethink how we see some of the words John uses here. When John refers to the *servants of God*, we need to understand his context. John referred to himself as a *servant of God* in Chapter 1:1. John was not martyred, and he was called a servant or actually a slave of God, just like the 144,000. Sealing of the slaves or servants of God continues throughout the entire Bible and even continues through today. Many have said this is a reference to only Jewish believers. I think they do that to push home their opinion of pre-trib, mid-trib, post-trib, and the catching away, which many call the rapture. Pre, mid, or post-trib do not need our help by using ideas with no biblical background. **We also cannot realistically say that God's servants that have been sealed are in need of resealing.**

Looking through the Bible we see many who were called servants or slaves of God such as Moses, David, Gideon, Deborah, Josiah, the list is almost endless. None of these died as martyrs, but were called slaves/servants of God long before this vision occurred in 95 AD.

So, could some say that there are two or three different kinds of sealed servants/slaves of God? The 144,000 and then the others? <u>Of course not</u>. When we become God's servant, we are sealed. I believe that ALL of God's servants are being sealed even today, based upon the choices each one makes.

There are multiple places in the Bible that reference the seal of God, 2 *Corinthians 1:21-22*, *Ephesians 1:13-14*, and *Ephesians 4:30* are just a few. What happens when something is sealed? A seal protects an item from being tampered, it reveals an authenticity, it shows it belongs to someone, and anyone who is not authorized is not allowed to know what is in it. God ordered His servants to be sealed, protected, marked so everyone would know they were His.

The Multitude

John continues describing what he is seeing. After seeing the fifth angel with the seal, John sees before him a great multitude that was too many to count. This multitude came from every nation, tribe, people, and language, and they were standing before the throne and the Lamb. Again, this is symbolic as John is emphasizing a point. He describes the multitude as wearing white robes and holding palm branches in their hands as they cried out, *"Salvation belongs to our God, who sits on the throne, and to the Lamb"* (Revelation 7:9-10 NIV).

Each vision within the vision tells a part of the entire story. The multitude John sees is the church around the throne in heaven. The 144,000 are numbered on the earth, yet the multitude is not numbered in heaven. The 144,000 has been sealed without any mention of the rest of the number of heaven being sealed. The idea of 144,000 is a symbolic number and the sealing was done on earth. The idea of 144,000 has become more than it was intended. Many say that the 144,000 go through the great tribulation, and I have no problem with that. Could it be called the great tribulation because it is the first time since the flood that such a thing has covered the entire earth? It is very hard when you read the history of the world to see how any kind of tribulation could be worse than what has already taken place in the world. There have been famines, starvation, and decimating plagues, and they have existed in some form in every generation. In my opinion, the great tribulation will be a worldwide trial where no one is left out. With the exception of the great flood, nothing else I am aware of covered the entire world.

Great Tribulation

Let's consider *Revelation 6:4* again where John describes the fiery red horse, where its rider was given power to take peace from the earth and to make people kill each other. He was given a large sword. The word for *sword* here is a direct reference to the sword that the Roman soldiers carried every day, the *mac'haira*, a short 20" sword. It's not speaking about a large

Thracian sword that was 4' or longer carried into battle and slung from the shoulder.

When John mentions, "there was given to him a great sword," it means more death and destruction than was known previously by any typical ruler and army. **This "great tribulation" is only capitalized in the books that are written today. When the Bible was written, <u>it was not capitalized</u>, meaning we are the ones who have made this tribulation into more than was intended. There will be great tribulation just as Jesus said, but it will be one that includes everyone on the earth at that time, not something else.**

Then, one of the elders asked John a question, *"'John, do you know who these people are and where they came from?' John answered. 'Sir, you know.' And then the elder explained. Those are the ones who had come out of the great tribulation, who washed their robes and made them white in the blood of the Lamb"* (Revelation 7:13-14, Paraphrased).

Luke explains that a believer *must go through many hardships, many tribulations to enter the kingdom of God (Acts 14:22, Paraphrased)*. It seems to me that the church has created a new definition for the word tribulation, based upon a misunderstanding of the word in Revelation. The word tribulation means *anguish, persecution, and trouble*; <u>there is no mystique in this word</u>. It means what it means. We would be hard pressed to say one tribulation was greater and more damaging than another. For those who went through the plagues, famines, purgings, inquisitions, wars, and the like, would argue, justifiably, that what happened to them was unbearable. Remember though, this word written in Revelation was done in lower case letters. The term "great tribulation" is simply a reference to a tribulation that is in <u>greater dimension than before</u>, because no one will be excluded from this trial.

Then, the elder asked John, *"Who are in the white robes and where did they come from?"* John's answer from the original text was, *"My lord knows,"* and then when transcribed in the New International Version John's response was written as, *"Sir, you know."* A term of highest respect to one who is considered noble. Then, the elder said to John, *"These are the ones coming out of the great tribulation."* During this conversation, there is no time given, or chronological order or location for this statement. "Coming out of" is a present participle, without any reference to time. A present participle is a verb ending in "ing" that denotes continuous action. This word leads the reader to understand that those past, present, and even future are referred to here.

Consider with me all the tribulation periods of the past several thousand years, many of them lasting decades. Now look at the time referred to as the great tribulation, which lasts only three-and-a-half years. How can we suddenly exclude bubonic plague of Europe, the potato famine in Ireland, the Depression in America, the Russian Revolution, the Civil War, the Holocaust, the Inquisition, the Roman Coliseum, and the savagery of the arena, along with the saints mauled to death by lions, burned alive on posts to light the road for the emperor, being boiled alive in oil, dismembered and disemboweled. I bring all of these to your attention for one purpose, so that we have a grip on what is actual and not make it into something it is not. We cannot say that a three-and-a-half-year period could be worse for anyone than decades of what I said previously. This great multitude that John is seeing came from every generation, and to say they all came from this three-and-a-half-year period is not rational.

As the elder was describing the ones who are "coming out of the great tribulation," he explained that they had washed their robes and made them white in the blood of the Lamb. Let's look at this a little closer. The word "coming" gives the reader the key to understanding, and the intention of this verse. There has never been a time when tribulation is absent from the saints. Somewhere in this world at all times, not everywhere, but somewhere, today, there is tribulation. When the great tribulation comes, then it will be everywhere at the same time; that is why I believe it is called the great tribulation. All the tribulations of the past, present, and future are included in the words coming out of the great tribulation.

The elder continues explaining to John that those coming out of the great tribulation will have robes washed in the blood of the Lamb. <u>Where did the robes come from?</u> Why would you need to wash your robe? We have shared in time past that when we are born again, God gives us a new suit, all made in white. Isaiah explained this perfectly for us when he said, *"Wash and make yourselves clean. Take your evil deeds out of my sight; stop doing wrong. Learn to do right; seek justice. Defend the oppressed. Take up the cause of the fatherless; plead the case of the widow. Come now, let us settle the matter, says the Lord. Though your sins are like scarlet, they shall be as white as snow; though they are red as crimson, they shall be like wool" (Isaiah 1:16-18 NIV)*. Isaiah explains in these verses that at your born-again experience, you are given a new robe.

John writes, *"They cried out with a loud voice: 'Lord, the One who is holy and true, how long until You judge and avenge our blood from those who live on the earth?' So a white robe was given to each of them, and they were told to rest a little while longer until the number would be completed of their fellow slaves and their brothers, who were going to be killed just as they had been"* (Revelation 6:10-11 HCSB). It may not appear that robes are given at born-again experience, but that creates a question – in heaven – why would we need to wash our robes?

This applies to every generation. All who are His have robes dipped in Him. How does that work? You shed your blood for Christ, and He sheds His blood for you, and now you have become a martyr for the faith that you have. His red blood washes you and makes your robe white. How does red blood make your robe white? This only happens with God. The aorist tense states past facts, *what has already occurred*, and it can be continuing, it could mean they washed and whitened, removing soil, tarnish, stains that had gotten on their robes from the time they accepted Jesus as Savior and Lord. <u>This is all symbolic</u>. The robes are a symbol of our relationship with Christ. Only the blood of Christ can make us holy and allow us to wear white robes, a symbol of purity. As we live on this earth, we are always getting soiled in some manner, whether through anger, hatred, bigotry, complaining, jealousy, vengeance, bitterness, just to name a few. Our soul man is alive, and our spirit man is far from being what he should be, even here on the earth. Those who wash their robes in the blood of the Lamb are the ones who come out of the tribulation in our time here on earth to eternal glory in heaven. <u>This is all who have remained true to Christ, including the martyrs.</u>

Around the Throne

After the elder describes those coming out of the great tribulation, he then proceeds to explain what will happen to them. *Once their robes are washed and made white by the blood of the Lamb, they will be before the throne of God serving Him day and night in His temple; and He who sits on the throne will shelter them with His presence. They will never hunger or thirst again. The sun will not beat down on them, nor any scorching heat. For the Lamb at the center of the throne will be their shepherd; He will lead them to springs of living water. And God will wipe away every tear from their eyes (Revelation 7:15-17, Paraphrased).* Nothing from history can pass into where John and they are now. Not hunger from famine and starvation, not thirst, and not heat. These are symbols of tribulation, hardships that the Israelites <u>and Christians</u> have faced. The terminology that John uses does not do it justice, yet it is the appropriate terminology, as it is the only thing we could understand. We have not yet received our heavenly words that would describe all of this in its magnitude.

Remember, John is seeing this from the viewpoint of Jesus. Jesus is revealing it all to John. At this point, the entire church is before the throne, no one is further away than any other. Can you imagine a devoted father with seven children telling two to come close and the other five to stay behind? Of course not, yet many must believe that, since that is how we hear these scriptures read and taught. All are near the father in relationship and essence especially since, there is no time and space considerations in heaven. When John uses the word *temple*, we need to remember that it is <u>not a place</u>, <u>not a building</u> of some kind, but a symbol of our meeting and being together in heaven. There is no need for a temple since we have already become His temple.

John said after they were dressed in robes of white, they will be before the throne of God serving Him day and night. Did

I miss something, or does it say, *"they all serve Him day and night?"* It sounds like John is describing a group that jumped ahead to serve God day and night while the rest of us just fit in the best we can. That concept is hard to accept, and it forgets who He is, and what we all are to Him. Of course, we all know *there is no day and night in heaven (Revelation 22:4-5)*. So, John was speaking symbolically.

Another interesting thought to consider is when John saw the sixth seal open, there were a multitude of events that occurred including *the stars that fell from the sky (Revelation 6:13)*. So, there was no light coming from the stars to make a determination as to whether it was day or night. And, in *Revelation 22:5*, John tells us that God will be our light. We will not need the light of the sun or a lamp.

John explains that the Lamb who is at the center of the throne will be their shepherd. He will lead them to springs of living water, and He will wipe all the tears from their eyes.

We can only look at this verse through the eyes of humanity. Water, food, and fountains are only human terms to express the glory of being with Christ. They are symbolic and cannot touch the reality of that glory.

John has just been placed in a scene where there are no more tears, means two things. First, no more trouble that can create tears, and second, no memory of past hurt, circumstances, or the memory of those who did not make it to heaven. The memory of them must be erased or there would be tears. *Psalm 126:5 (NIV)*, *"Those who sow with tears will reap with songs of joy."*

THE SEVENTH SEAL AND THE GOLDEN CENSER

CHAPTER 14

Can you imagine being in a world where noise was all around you? You could hear the birds singing, the water flowing in the creeks, dogs barking, crickets chirping, music playing, etc., and then in an instant it all went silent? You could hear nothing. This is what John experienced in his vision in heaven when the seventh seal was opened. There was *30 minutes of silence*, it must have felt like a lifetime, an eternity *(Revelation 8:1)*. Of course, John was not wearing a watch, but 30 minutes in heaven with no sound must have been a long time to John. There was no other seal opened with such presentation and feeling of awe. And yet, they were overwhelming and substantive to us. Think of yourself in John's situation, what would silence do to you? It's hard for us to simply stand in silence for 10 minutes during a church service.

For some, it's very overwhelming. That's because silence increases tension; it sets us on edge; anticipation is heightened. It raises questions upon questions in our minds. John has never experienced such silence before, it was so deafening; he could hear it beating in his ears.

At this point in the vision, John is revealing the prophetic outcome of the life of Jesus, His death and resurrection as the Lamb who was slain, the conclusion of the time on earth as we know it. All the sealed words have been revealed and the last seal is now opened.

John does not give us a chronological order of the seventh seal. Therefore, we are unsure where it fits within the vision.

Prayer and Incense

Go back with me to *Revelation 4:1* when Jesus tells John, *"Come up here John and I will show you what must occur after these dealings with the seven churches" (HCSB)*. After John watches what happens to the seven churches, he enters heaven and is now in the spirit. Everything we have seen, heard, and read are revealed to John while he is in the spirit *(Revelation 1:10; 4:1-2)*. A natural man could not receive or handle what John is viewing, it is all of a spiritual nature.

Within the visions, John has already revealed the destruction of the four horsemen, the martyrs, and the seal brings us to the door that leads to the very end. Here is where John sees seven angels, not archangels, but regular angels, each holding a trumpet, who have been given a special assignment. Their assignments were written upon a scroll that was sealed with seven seals. I can see the seals going down the scroll, one after the other. The seal below the first one was not visible until after the first angel completed the task assigned to him. Once the angel's assignment was completed, the next seal was revealed, and opened by the Lamb and so on until all seven angels completed their assignments.

John continues to watch the scenes unfold before him. He is once again seeing a vision within a vision. In this portion, he does not mention any of the others we saw in the other scenes, only the throne, which is symbolic of God's power and dominion. He begins here describing *another angel who came and stood at the altar with a gold incense burner. He was given a large amount of incense to offer with the prayers of all the saints on the gold altar in front of the throne. The smoke from the incense, with the prayers of the saints, went up in the presence of God from the angel's hand (Revelation 8:3-4, Paraphrased).* The term used for "another angel" reminds us of the angel who commanded the four angels to keep the winds completely still. This angel is carrying a censor, which is a vessel for burning incense. Keep in mind the censor and the altar are both made of gold. I believe it's because of the value of what is in it.

The golden altar appears right in front of the throne, it cannot be missed. The smoke and prayers of the saints are rising before the throne. This is not like the altar of incense in the tabernacle on the earth, where the priests had to throw live coals on the incense to make the smoke rise. These prayers are ascending as the angel is increasing the incense to that, which is rising before the presence of God. The intensity is beyond anything we could ever comprehend. What if incense is intercession? What if it is worship? Just a thought. Incense burns as smoke, which creates a pleasant, visible odor before the Lord. I wonder why it was necessary to be visible.

Then, "*the angel took the incense burner, filled it with fire from the altar, and hurled it to the earth; there were rumblings of thunder, flashes of lightning, and an earthquake. And the seven angels who had the seven trumpets prepared to blow them*" *(Revelation 8:5-6 HCSB)*. John said that the angel threw the incense burner into the earth, <u>and not the incense</u>; that went up before the throne of God, then the angel filled the censor with fire from the altar of incense and threw fire to the earth.

Does this represent God's answers to the prayers of His saints? Is this a symbol of the answers from God to the prayers mixed with incense? I say that, because after this censor of fire is thrown into the earth, the angels unleash hell. Those who appeared at the altar of sacrifice no longer have to wait for their deaths to be avenged by God. All the prayers of the saints that have not yet been answered are being addressed.

God has proven time and time again in His Word that when He sends judgment upon the earth, He does it as a warning that there is little time left before the end before there is NO more time to repent. It's His shot across the bow. This vision John is seeing is one of those times. It is just about the end, and God is giving people a chance to repent. Then, *the angel threw the censor to the earth, it rocked the world as "every mountain and island was moved from its place" (Revelation 6:14, Paraphrased).* This was way more than just an earthquake. Earthquake here means *great and terrible shaking.* It was so intense that all the rulers of the earth, military commanders, the rich and powerful, and *every slave and free person hid in caves and among the rocks of the mountains crying out for the rocks to fall on them and hide them from the face of God (Revelation 6:16, Paraphrased).* It was absolute terror. These people <u>were not</u> born-again believers.

Supernatural Occurrences

Looking back through Bible history, we see a judgment in Ezekiel that was foretold by God. This judgment was against Russia, Gog, and all that had come with them to attack Israel. God said, *"I will execute judgment on him [Russia, Gog] with plague and bloodshed. I will pour out torrential rain, hailstones, fire, and brimstone on him, as well as his troops and the many peoples who are with him"* (Ezekiel 38:22 HCSB).

And again, look further back in history when God dealt with Pharaoh in Egypt where Pharaoh did not believe in any god greater than himself, which is very similar to mankind today. In Egypt, God made promises to Abraham, Jacob, and Isaac when God said, *"I will bring you to the land that I swore to give to Abraham, Isaac, and Jacob, and I will give it to you as a possession.*

I am Yahweh" (Exodus 6:8 HCSB). Here the slavery of Israel as a nation comes to an end. As Moses was being obedient to God, He had *Moses stretch forth his staff toward heaven and the Lord sent thunder and hail. Lightning struck the earth and the Lord rained hail on the land of Egypt. The hail and lightning were so severe that nothing like it had occurred in the land of Egypt, since it had become a nation. The hail struck down everything in the field, both man and beast, and it beat down every plant in the field and shattered every tree (Exodus 9:23-25 KJV, Paraphrased)*. This was no ordinary storm.

Let's look forward for just a minute to see what happens when the seventh angel blew his trumpet. *There were loud voices in heaven proclaiming that the kingdom of the world has become the [kingdom] of our Lord and of His Messiah, and He will reign forever and ever! (Revelation 11:15, Paraphrased)* At this point, <u>it's over</u>! This takes us to the end and explains the timing.

As you can see NONE of this is a reference to the past as this appears to be ahead of us. ALL is yet to come, or is it? Is some of this taking place right now?

Going back to John's revelation, while the first angel was preparing and working through his assignment, the other 6 angels had been waiting for an order, before they blew their trumpets. Once the censor hit the earth, all seven angels prepared to blow, however, a period of months passed between the blowing of each of the trumpets. When *the first angel blew his trumpet, hail and fire, mixed with blood, were hurled to the earth. At this point, a third of the earth, trees, and green grass, including crops, were all burned up (Revelation 8:6-7, Paraphrased)*. There was horrible destruction after the first trumpet was blown, a supernatural judgment, which God has recorded, but notice, no one was recorded as having been killed. It was not until the 3rd trumpet sounds that men are mentioned, and in the 5th men are killed. It was not a natural occurrence; it was a warning. Each shot gets closer and closer to the end, which is a lot like a shot going across the bow of a ship that falls and strikes the ship but does not destroy or sink it.

Another supernatural judgment occurred *when God told Moses to stretch his hand toward heaven and hail would fall throughout the land of Egypt. God rained hail on the land of Egypt as lightning that struck the earth. It was so severe that nothing like it had occurred in the land of Egypt since it had become a nation. The hail struck down everything in its path, including every plant and tree of the field, and both man and beast. The only place it didn't hail was in the land of Goshen where the Israelites were living (Exodus 9:18-26, Paraphrased).*

This supernatural phenomenon was very extreme, because it does not rain in Egypt, much less hail. In central and southern Egypt, several years may pass without any measurable rain. When it does come, it is very brief and sometimes, but rarely, a downpour will occur creating flood conditions. On an average, the rainfall in a good year in northern Egypt is 7.9 inches but decreases as you head south. The weather station at Giza kept a record of rainfall from 1931 to 1986, a total of 672 months, 56 years, revealing less than one inch of rain per year at that location.

Judgments

The progression of the judgments as the trumpets were blown reveal that the first judgment created a famine. However, this is not the first famine that was brought by the pale or livid or green horse and rider. So, what kind of famine is this? It obviously is not a new famine of food. Could this be a <u>famine of the word of God</u>?

The 2nd trumpet takes away trade and commerce in one-third of the world. The 3rd and 4th are combined horror. This is not as some write, the destruction of Jerusalem, which has already occurred or some invasion by enemy armies. The six judgments show increased horror and destruction, much like the 10 plagues God put on Egypt when Pharaoh was ruler. Each plague got worse each time. This same kind of destruction and horror will come on those remaining on the earth during the last days.

The phrase "**those remaining** upon the earth" does not refer to Christians. This is about the earth – it is unnecessary to say, "those remaining," unless they are singled out.

Recall the events surrounding the ten plagues of Egypt. The chosen people of God suffered during the first three plagues, which included, the Nile River running with blood, dead frogs everywhere, and then biting lice on their bodies. These three plagues affected everyone. It was not until the fourth plague that the Israelites were separated from Egypt *(Exodus 8:21-23)*. Each plague was worse and created more aftermath than the one before it. They were merely an example of the seven trumpets and the judgment that comes with them during the worldwide tribulation. Keep in mind there is no chronological order given for the blowing of the trumpets.

We know when the first trumpet blew it was horrible, and the rest gradually more horrible. This judgment or tribulation is upon the entire world; no one is left out. *When the first angel blew his trumpet, hail and fire, mixed with blood were hurled to the earth.*

A third of the earth, including trees and grass were burned up (Revelation 8:7, Paraphrased). If the third of the world's trees were hit, did it happen all in one location or over the span of various locations? There is no sure answer, but I would think that this judgment has fallen on some very specific area or areas. It was so bad and intense that one third of all the vegetation of the earth was destroyed. As the second angel blew his trumpet, something like a great mountain ablaze with fire was hurled into the sea. What would this create, something like a mountain physically thrown into the sea? It would create a tsunami affecting numerous islands, coastlines, and countries, knocking them off of their set boundaries. As the boundaries shift, damage would be irreversible, famine and destruction everywhere, infrastructure in chaos, and death rampant. GPS would no longer work.

There has never been anything close to this in history with such worldwide reaching affects. All previous tsunamis have been localized in region or a territory but did not touch the world.

John describes the effects upon the earth, when he explains how *"a third of the sea became blood, a third of the living creatures in the sea died, and a third of the ships were destroyed"* (Revelation 8:8-9 HCSB). Some commentators have said this was a volcano. If this were a volcano, we would not see one third of the sea turned to blood. A volcano is localized and the red of the lava as it cools, changes color, and turns black soon after it hits the water. It may travel hundreds of yards, but not thousands of miles or even 10 miles. The effects of a volcano, however, can travel many thousand miles and have terrible effects on the earth. Volcanos can create tsunamis, and the smoke and ash from the volcano cause darkness for miles and can last for months on end. Mt. St. Helens did exactly that in 1986. It even affected the weather.

In the book of Exodus, we see where the Nile River was turned to blood *(Exodus 7:17-18)*. We know that blood means blood, and in Revelation we see that one third of the sea became blood. In Revelation, the water became blood and that caused the fish to die and the mammals in that area to die. However, all the fish in this area could die, but that still would not cause the sea to be blood. In these verses, God has written that this is how mankind will know that God is in the middle of this, and He is in the midst of what is taking place. So, what happens to shipping, commerce, and fishing in that area? At the very least, one third ceases to exist. This is judgment, and it is far greater than what happened to the Nile River. Tens of thousands of miles of oceans turned to blood.

Then, *"the third angel blew his trumpet, and a great star, blazing like a torch, fell from heaven. It fell on a third of the rivers and springs of water. The name of the star is [Absinthos or] Wormwood"* (Revelation 8:10-11a HCSB). In Russian, Wormwood is Chernoble. This star was bigger than the mountain like object that was hurled into the ocean. *"Many of the people died from the waters, because the waters had been made bitter"* (Revelation 8:10-11 HCSB). Notice that when the third angel blew the trumpet, a star fell from heaven. This star affects the rivers and springs of water. Was this over all the earth or just in a certain location? Notice that this star has a name – Wormwood.

When the star fell into the waters, a third of the water became wormwood. Is this a reference to a specific star? Maybe it was a comet or meteorite. Regardless, many people died, because of the Wormwood.

Jeremiah prophesied this would happen, *"Therefore, this is what the Lord of Hosts, the God of Israel, says: 'I am about to feed this people wormwood and give them poisonous water to drink.'"* (Jeremiah 9:15 HCSB) Why did God say He would feed them wormwood? *The people had abandoned God's instruction, stopped listening to His voice, and refused to walk with Him. Their hearts were stubborn and they followed in their father's ways of Baal* (Jeremiah 9:13-14, Paraphrased). Because of this, they were going to recap the whirlwind of God's wrath.

Recall the ways of Balaam in Numbers 22-31. He was the man who taught the enemies of God how to trip up and bring death and destruction to Israel. Balak, the king of Moab hired Balaam to use his prophetic gift to pronounce and prophesy against Israel, because Balak was afraid of Israel. But every time Balaam tried to curse, He ended up blessing Israel instead. Balaam kept trying to curse Israel with no success. Finally, in a desperate move, he told Balak to entice Israel to intermarry the women of Moab. This became the trap that destroyed many of them. This trap is not one that catches and later one can be released from. This trap catches and kills. It was what Jesus referred to in *Revelation 2:14*. Balaam's suggestions and encouragement were well received, because he was well respected by the people for his prophetic gift. Therefore, Israel moved upon them and intermarried with Moab, against God's previous command, which polluted the entire nation.

Is this judgment from the third angel, because of this behavior found all over the world? One third of all fresh water is burnt up. For America, <u>could this be</u> throwing down our Constitution, which is based upon biblical truths, for man's perverted ideas of abortion and same sex marriage and on and on? Is Wormwood false teaching and preaching in the church – like Balaam and Jezebel? This behavior is disrespecting the foundations of our beliefs and riding roughshod over them for gain. We might want to pause and consider that.

Let's recap. The first angel took one third of the earth by fire. The second, took one third of the ocean by fire. The third angel took one third of the waters of the earth. Now only two-thirds of all water remains in the world.

Next, *"the fourth angel blew his trumpet and a third of the sun was struck, a third of the moon, and a third of the stars, so that a third of them were darkened. A third of the day was without light, and the night as well"* (Revelation 8:12 HCSB). When this trumpet sounded, one third of the sun, moon, and stars went out; one third of all light for day and night were suddenly gone. Eight additional hours added to the other hours of darkness. Darkness so thick you can feel it, so thick you are afraid to move. The word for darkness here is *skotos*, which means moral darkness.

Keep in mind that *Revelation 6:14* told us that the stars had already fallen. If they had fallen, they can't fall again, so, this must be symbolic. We were also told in Revelation 6 that the unripe figs were blown off the trees by the wind. This does not happen. The wind does not affect green figs whatsoever. Only rotten or damaged figs fall off the trees. Does this mean it is symbolic? If so, what does it mean?

Have you ever heard someone say, "I feel an ill wind blowing?" This saying had nothing to do with a breeze or a wind – nothing at all. This wind was referring to a wind of change, a sense of trouble or foreboding or something of that order. What if the wind that caused the stars to drop to the ground like unripe figs <u>was a change in ideology</u> – in a belief that one held and now has changed his mind?

Consider with me, the Presbyterians, Lutherans, Methodists, and other denominations that began as reformers, following hard after Christ. They have allowed a wind of change to cause them to drop like figs, and no longer have anything real and lasting to offer anyone in need. Many have become diminished from the redeeming qualities that a church must have. They can only follow the patterns of man. These patterns have taken from them the one thing that mattered – the words of God and Christ that will impact and change lives from the inside out. Now, having blended in with society and produced a social message, and not a redeeming message, they have little real value to the cross of Christ. They now walk in partial darkness and create more darkness, because they no longer accurately follow Christ. They follow man's programs and man-made ideologies, and as they compromised the word of God. **They cannot speak about the blood of Christ or holiness because these are not social messages, and those two words stir the pot and the fence sitters.** The fence sitters will not challenge anyone, because it is not seeker or socially friendly or politically correct. They preach about social reform and programs without the power of Christ. They exclude Christ and His laws and tolerate any and all sin with the words, "we must not condemn, and we must be inclusive." They have a form of godliness but deny the power of God is for today. We are instructed to stay away from those who present themselves as, *"...having a form of godliness but denying its power. Have nothing to do with such people"* (2 *Timothy 3:5 NIV*).

They are dying spiritually and many of their words are dead from the heart up and head down. If Christ has condemned evil and sin, then we must follow his pattern, not the condemnation of the person, but the rejection of the sin and the continued practice of the sin. We must teach the better way.

Could the stars be one third of the ministers who have fallen from God's grace or those who have forgotten their first love? <u>Is this symbolic</u> of the darkness people enjoy, because of their sins? Is this spiritual darkness? Jesus is the light and without Him there is no light. Is this the absence of truth? Could be. When people believe a lie, will they move easily to believe another lie? Then another and another. The more lies that are accepted, the more lies that are created, and the more the people walk in darkness.

Amos describes exactly what is taking place in Revelation about the loss of daylight hours. He also addressed why it was occurring, which was because of the people's attitude of sin and selfishness *(Amos 8:4-12)*. Amos is given revelation by God. God tells Amos what is coming, because of the behavior and practices of the Jews. He explains that there will be a <u>famine</u> throughout the land, not of bread or water, <u>but of hearing the words of the Lord</u>.

I believe we have been on the cusp of this taking place. As long as the church and major groups within the church will allow the word to be stripped of its intent and lose what the gospel intends for us to know and live, we are on a downhill collision course with the living God and His wrath, and the Lamb that was slain. The famine of the word is coming, and it is coming soon. Even now there are many places where it is difficult to hear anything, but a social gospel, a gospel without Christ. Many are preaching a gospel that accepts the sinner, and allows him to keep his sin, and not teaching the sinner must turn from his sin. Matthew explained this behavior: *"Then the disciples came up and asked Him, 'Why do you speak to them in parables?' He answered them, 'Because the secrets of the kingdom of heaven have been given for you to know, but it has not been given to them. For whoever has [more] will be given to him, and he will have more than enough, but whoever does not have, even what he has will be taken away from him. For this reason, I speak to them in parables, because looking they do not see, and hearing they do not listen or understand. Isaiah's prophecy is fulfilled in them, which says: You will listen and listen, yet never understand; and you will look and look, yet never perceive"* (Matthew 13:10-14 HCSB). Matthew was explaining that people can watch and listen to Jesus, but because they rejected Him in their hearts, they are not capable of understanding the truth. Those who refuse and reject Him will lose what they have and move quickly into darkness and more darkness. This is a preamble to the judgment that is coming in Revelation, so, could this fourth angel be describing the delusions of closed minds to the gospel, increased by their own evil, creating more darkness? Could be.

As John sees another angel, and watches as things transpire, he is reminded of what Isaiah saw when he described that very moment when he saw the Lord seated on a high and lofty throne, and His robe filled the temple. Isaiah scribed the most magnificent scene before him, as he visualized the Seraphim standing above Him, each one calling to the other: *Holy, holy, holy is the Lord of Hosts; His glory fills the whole earth. At the very sound of their voices, the foundations of the doorways shook, and the temple was filled with smoke (Isaiah 6:1-4, Paraphrased).*

Could it be the smoke that filled the temple was incense before the throne that burns in the censor going before the Lord into the nostrils of God, which John was seeing in his revelation? John described an angel appeared bringing with him a gold incense burner standing at the altar. He was given a large amount of incense to offer with the prayers of all the saints on the gold altar in front of the throne. The smoke of the incense, with the prayers of the saints, went up in the presence of God from the angel's hand. The angel took the incense burner, filled it with fire from the altar, and hurled it to the earth; there were rumblings of thunder, flashes of lightning, and an earthquake [a terrible and great shaking].

Again, in Isaiah's conversation with God about Israel, he heard the voice of the Lord saying: *"Who should I send? Who will go for Us?" Isaiah replied, "Here I am. Send me." The Lord replied: "Go! Say to these people: Keep listening, but do not understand; keep looking, but do not perceive. Dull the minds of these people; deafen their ears and blind their eyes; otherwise they might see with their eyes and hear with their ears, understand with their minds, turn back, and be healed"* (Isaiah 6:8-10 HCSB). Israel had removed and forsaken God. So, God sent an angel to help them do what they prefer to do in God's face. In Revelation, the same thing occurred. Man has forsaken and removed God.

John's attention is directed to an eagle flying high and crying out very loudly, *"Woe! Woe! Woe to those who live on the earth, because of the remaining trumpet blasts that the three angels are about to sound!"* (Revelation 8:13b HCSB) <u>The definition of woe</u> is a condition of suffering from misfortune, affliction, or grief. It includes calamity and economic woes.

To get a better picture of the word "woe", recall the life of Job, to whom Satan brought woes. He lost his children, his home, health, wealth, his place, and position in the city, as well as his hopes and dreams.

At this point, four judgments have come and three woes of the three trumpets from the three angels have yet to sound. Keep in mind that when we see the term, *"those dwelling or living on the earth,"* references <u>those who remain upon the earth</u>, who have rejected Christ and His gospel, and chosen the way of the world instead. In my opinion, after chapter 3 of Revelation, the church is no longer in the earth. They appear to be in heaven around the throne. So, they are not affected by these judgments. Just a reminder for you, <u>Jesus said</u> His church would not be tested in the tribulation that would cover the entire world. *"Since you have kept my command to endure patiently, I will also keep you from the hour of trial that is going to come on the whole world to test the inhabitants of the earth. I am coming soon. Hold on to what you have, so that no one will take your crown"* (Revelation 3:10-11 NIV).

The eagle John is seeing was flying in the midst, or in the middle heavens as some translations say. Apparently, he is flying just high enough to make his declaration over the whole world in case someone was listening. However, it seems that only John was listening, as the whole world had rejected Christ and His ways, because the world was not listening.

Again, as we are revealing and seeing the seven seals open, we are not given any chronological order for the placement of this vision. This could be happening now, even as we speak.

John's visions portrayed what was going to come. Looking back at the very beginning of this vision, we see that Jesus told John what he was about to see was the now and what will take place later *(Revelation 1:19, Paraphrased)*.

The revelation was given to John, so he would know what would take place suddenly and with swiftness. Everyone wants to know when things are going to happen – when will the end come, what is going to happen before the end comes, what do we as the church do, and where are we in all of this? It is part of our nature to ask when will these things take place, or as each of us has heard our children say, "Daddy, are we there yet?"

THE TRUMPETS CONTINUE

CHAPTER 15

Have you ever had a dream where you were in the midst of watching things unfold before you, and the longer the dream went, the more intense it got? This is the point where John is in his vision. The intensity is beyond imagination. There is no way John could imagine any of this on his own. *At this point in John's vision, the fifth angel blows his trumpet, and John <u>saw a star</u> that had fallen from heaven to earth. The key to the shaft of the abyss was given to the angel who opened the abyss. When he did, smoke came up out of the shaft like smoke from a great furnace, so that the sun and the air were darkened by the smoke (Revelation 9:1-2, Paraphrased).*

Keep in mind that we already read about the sixth seal and what happened when it was opened as well as the other seals. The sun turned black as sackcloth of hair, one third of the sun no longer shined, the moon turned to blood, and all the stars fell to the earth, so what was John describing at this point in his vision? What does it mean? Who gave the angel the key to Hades, the abyss? *"I was dead, but look – I am alive forever and ever, and I hold the keys of death and Hades" (Revelation 1:18 HCSB).* <u>Jesus holds the keys</u>, and He is the one who gave the key to the angel. This is not a natural phenomenon; this is spiritual.

The Woes

John continues to describe what is happening. Arising out of the abyss was smoke that carried locusts to the earth. The shape of the locusts was like a horse that had been prepared for battle. Upon their head was something like a gold crown, and their faces were like that of men. They had hair as that of a woman, teeth like a lion, a chest like an iron breastplate, and the sound of their wings was like the sound of chariots with many horses rushing into battle.

Their tails carried stingers like scorpions with the power to harm people for five months. They had a king, who was the angel of the abyss. His name in Hebrew was Abaddon, and in Greek he has the name Apollyon, which means destroyer. This was the first woe. There were still two more woes to come after this (Revelation 9:10-12, Paraphrased). Power was given to them like the power that scorpions have on the earth. *The locusts were told not to harm the grass, any green plant, or tree upon the earth, but only people who did not have God's seal on their forehead. They were only permitted to torment like a scorpion when it strikes a man, sting and inflict pain upon the people. In these days, people will seek death, but will not be able to find it. They will long to die, but death will not come to them (Revelation 9:3-6, Paraphrased).*

The description of the locust that John describes is so intense, that he broke it down so the reader would understand exactly what he was seeing. He described the locust like that of a horse, a man, and even a woman. The horses were described as equipped for battle, which means that this group was organized for war. It was not a mob or a wild uncontrolled group. They wore crowns and had faces similar to men. This tells me they had the ability to think, so that they could differentiate between the sealed and those who were not sealed. They wore armor and had tails like a scorpion and could sting for five months. <u>Since when</u> do locusts or any other bug have a leader or one with a name? In the natural, locust swarm and do not have a leader. Thus, we can see that this is a picture with spiritual implications. This is the first woe that came with the sound of the fifth angel.

Interesting that the locusts were only allowed to torment those people for five months who did not have God's seal. Five is the number that means halfway <u>or incomplete</u>, and also is the number of grace. If you think that's strange, then you must understand that God's grace is being extended to these men, so they will repent before He completes this tribulation. God's purpose is to give opportunity for repentance. The torture will be so intense that people will wish they were dead, yet they cannot die. If someone jumped out of a 20-story building, they would not die. If they threw themselves into a woodchipper, they would not die. If they threw themselves into the mouth of a shark, they would not die. Get the picture? In the natural, any of the events would result in death. So, what Jesus is saying to John is <u>this is spiritual</u> in its intent.

At the point of the sixth angel blowing his trumpet, four angels were released who were bound at the great river Euphrates. Very interesting that the four angels were restrained in the Great River Euphrates. This river was known to be the seat of great conquering nations such as Assyria, Babylon, and Persia. These four angels were waiting for the hour, day, month, and year to kill a third of the human race. The angels released a strong army of 200 million *(Revelation 9:13-16)*.

The four angels were instructed to kill one third of all men over a period of 13 months. At this time, there were about 6 billion people remaining on the earth. One-third is about two billion people. Remember, one quarter of all men were already killed, which was about two billion. So, half of the population of the earth had already been killed by this time, and yet those that remained upon the earth still refused to repent.

As John describes the scene, he does not distinguish between men and women as the word he used for *men* in this verse is *anthropos*, which means both men and women, however, if he meant only men, he probably would have used the word, *homoin*.

John's description of the army was intricate. *He saw horses that had horsemen who wore breastplates that were fiery red, hyacinth blue, and sulfur yellow. The heads of the horses were like a lion's head, which means they had teeth like lions, and from their mouths came fire, smoke, and sulfur. Their tails resembled snakes and had heads on them, and they inflicted injury. The power of the horses was in their mouths and tails (Revelation 9:17-19, Paraphrased).* Notice that John said their tails inflicted injury. It did not kill. The horses killed one third of the human race with their mouths using the three plagues – fire, smoke, and sulfur. <u>The horses kill</u> with their mouths, and not with their lion like teeth, <u>because this army is a demon army</u>.

For years, we have been told that this army was an army from Russia or China, yet notice that not one single shot, sword, spear, rifle, or any weapon killed anyone. It doesn't even say that the horsemen killed anyone. The horses are the ones who killed one third of the human race. <u>So, this is not an earthly army</u>. This is not Armageddon.

This supernatural demon army killed mankind without distinction of sex. This army is one that has yet to be revealed to the world just like the demon locusts that came in the fifth woe.

Often in today's society, scholars, pastors, commentators try very hard to understand Revelation and help others understand what John was seeing. However, their interpretations are devised erroneously as they try to modernize what John was seeing to relate it to today's world. Doing so is a failure to understand the purpose of Revelation, as well as incorrect exegesis. Remember, John is describing what Jesus is revealing to him. John is not conjuring up these things. If John saw tanks, he would have said they had wheels, and if there were helicopters, Jesus would have given John the correct words to describe them. What John described were demons, yet to be released upon the earth. The question is, "When?"

These spiritual occurrences are given as natural events to explain the unexplainable. John was told <u>what was</u> taking place and <u>what will</u> take place. And that is what he was to write in the Revelation given to him by Jesus.

One of the saddest things about this point in John's revelation is the fact that *the rest of the people who were not killed by these plagues <u>did not repent</u> of the works of their hands to stop worshiping demons and idols of gold, silver, bronze, stone, and wood, that were not able to see, hear, or walk (Revelation 9:20 HCSB).* The word idols here refer to the works of their own hands. They continued doing what they had been doing even though people around them had died. They did not change and turn from their wicked ways.

Made in the USA
Columbia, SC
19 April 2025